THE
leafygr

cookbook

THE
leafygreens
cookbook

100 Creative,
Flavorful Recipes
Starring Super-Healthy
Kale, Chard, Spinach,
Bok Choy, Collards
and More!

Kathryn Anible

 Ulysses Press

Published by: Ulysses Press
P.O. Box 3440
Berkeley, CA 94703
www.ulyssespress.com

ISBN: 978-1-61243-177-2
Library of Congress Catalog Number 2013931792

Printed in the United States by Bang Printing

10 9 8 7 6 5 4 3 2 1

Acquisitions editor: Keith Riegert
Project editor: Lauren Harrison
Editor: Phyllis Elving
Proofreader: Lauren Harrison
Interior design and layout: what!design @ whatweb.com
Front cover design: Rebecca Lown
Back cover design: what!design @ whatweb.com
Cover photos: *front:* © Anna Hoychuk/shutterstock.com
    back: sautéed kale © Andi Berger/shutterstock.com; pizza © Dream79/
    shutterstock.com; salmon © rakratchada/shutterstock.com; smoothie
    © Bartosz Luczak/shutterstock.com
Interior illustrations: © dayzeren/shutterstock.com
Index: Sayre Van Young

To my mother and my friends, who were inspirations for many recipes and were kind enough to taste my concoctions and give feedback.

tableofcontents

.

Introduction

Welcome to the wonderful world of leafy greens! No longer confined to just salads, leafy greens can be a part of every meal—and with over 100 varieties of greens available, you never risk becoming bored. This book is full of recipes that are easy to prepare and family friendly. Although only a fraction of those 100-plus greens are used in these recipes, some may be unfamiliar.

Getting to Know Your Greens

Arugula

Mildly spicy, this green is most commonly used in Italian cuisine. Mature plants have elongated and spiky leaves, while younger plants may resemble spinach. The younger, smaller leaves are milder in flavor.

Beet Greens

Maroon and dark green, this leafy green is typically sold attached to a bunch of beets. It has a mild flavor, similar to that of Swiss chard or spinach, and sometimes can even be a little sweet.

Belgian Endive

Crisp, bitter leaves are tightly packed in a rocket shape. The base is white and the leaves become yellow or very pale green near the tip. The greener the tip, the more bitter the flavor. Belgian endive is related to curly endive and escarole but has a more assertive flavor.

Bok Choy

A Chinese cabbage with a mild flavor and hearty texture, this green is most commonly used in Asian cuisines. Its stems should be bright white and the leaves bright to dark green.

Butterhead, Boston, or Bibb

This lettuce forms a head and is often sold in plastic clamshells to protect the delicate leaves. With a very mild, sweet flavor and leaves that form a bowl shape, bibb lettuce is best used in salads or for wraps.

Brussels Sprouts

These look and taste like little green cabbages. Look for sprouts that are firm and have tightly packed leaves. Smaller sprouts will have the best flavor and texture.

Cabbage

Savoy, green, and red cabbages are all similar in flavor, with the biggest differences coming from texture and color. Savoy cabbage is often very pale green with wrinkled leaves. Green and red cabbages are the same, except for color. Always look for heads that are heavy and have tightly packed leaves.

Cabbage, Napa

Also known as Chinese cabbage, this variety is long and oval, like a head of romaine. The leaves are wrinkled and pale green, and the flavor is milder than that of the red or green cabbage varieties. Look for heads that are firm, tightly packed, heavy for their size, and free of yellow spots or browning.

Collards Greens

Long, broad, dark green leaves characterize these greens. Popular in Southern cuisine, collards are usually braised, boiled, or stewed because of their tough texture. In the spring, baby collards, which have a milder flavor and texture, may be sautéed like spinach. Common ingredient combinations include collard greens, ham hock, tomato, and vinegar. Collards can have a lot of dirt on them, so they need to be thoroughly cleaned before cooking. It's recommended to swish them around in a large bowl of water, changing the water, and repeating until the water is clear. Collards are high in vitamins A and C, as well as calcium.

Dandelion Greens

Sometimes called a weed, dandelion greens can be difficult to find in the grocery store. The leaves of commercial dandelion greens are about 2 feet long, dark green, and spiky edged. The flavor is mild in younger, smaller plants in spring, but becomes bitter in larger leaves. This green is commonly used in salads, but may also be sautéed.

Escarole

With its light green curly leaves, escarole may look like green leaf lettuce at first glance. Slightly bitter and a bit crunchy, it makes a nice addition to salads and soups. Its relative endive may be used as a substitute, if escarole is not available.

Kale

Thanks to the growing popularity of kale, several varieties are available in markets nowadays. Curly, Tuscan (also known as Lacinato or dinosaur), and Siberian kales all have thick stalks, which may be pale green to purple, and veiny leaves, which may be broad or narrow. The flavor is mild and may be cabbagelike, depending on the variety, although almost any variety may be used when a recipe calls for kale. The only exception is red flowering kale, which is very bitter and is generally used as an ornamental plant. Kale is an excellent source of vitamins A, C, and K.

Mustard Greens

These very peppery leaves are often used in Asian and Southern cuisines. Popular combinations with mustard greens include ham, onion, and garlic as well as garlic, soy sauce, and sesame oil. When purchasing mustard greens, look for leaves that are solid green with crisp, thin stems.

Radicchio

A bright maroon or burgundy, this leafy vegetable is an exception when it comes to greens in color. Its vibrant hues make it a common ingredient in raw salads to add a burst of color, and it is usually added in small amounts. It can also be cooked, which mellows its normally bitter flavor.

Rapini, aka Broccoli Raab

The name "broccoli raab" can be confusing, since this dark leafy green does not taste anything like broccoli, so it is referred to as rapini throughout this book. Its flavor more closely resembles that of its relatives turnip greens and cabbage, with a bitter or pungent flavor. Rapini has thick stems, dark broad leaves up to 3 inches long, and small broccoli-like florets, and is usually packed in bunches.

Romaine

Crisp, elongated leaves, with dark green to pale green leaves, romaine is a common lettuce in North America. It has a mild and sometimes sweet flavor. Not as nutrient dense as most other greens, it is still high in fiber and has small amounts of vitamins A and C, as well as some potassium. Romaine is commonly used in salads, but may also be sautéed, broiled, or braised.

Spinach

Featuring round or oval dark green leaves, spinach is famous as a regular part of Popeye's diet. Spinach has a mild flavor that tastes of chlorophyll or might be characterized as tasting "very green." It has a smooth and delicate texture, which makes it great for salads or for quickly sautéing. Look for leaves that are unblemished and unbruised with dark, even coloring. Spinach is a good source of vitamins A, C, and K as well as iron and potassium. It also contains a small amount of protein.

Swiss Chard, aka Chard

This green has shiny leaves that appear rippled or wavy and stalks that are pale green, magenta, orange, yellow, or pink. Related to beets, Swiss chart has a much milder flavor than beet greens. It may be cooked in a variety of ways, and the leaves can be added to raw salads. Look for crisp, firm leaves and stalks. The paler the stalk, the milder the flavor. Swiss chard is high in vitamins A, C, and K as well as copper and iron. It contains a small amount of protein.

Turnip Greens

Often overlooked, bitter-flavored turnip greens are popular in Southern cuisine. They are an affordable green which can be purchased on their own or with the turnips attached. The leaves are bright to dark green with slightly curly edges and pale stems. Look for greens that are uniform in color and on the smaller side, as they will have a slight sweetness. Turnip greens are extremely high in vitamins A, C, and K and folate, as well as containing calcium, iron, and some protein.

Watercress

This peppery green with small, round, bright green leaves is commonly used in salads, soups, and sauces. It is often sold in bunches. Watercress is incredibly delicate and should be used within 2 days of purchase. It is high in vitamins, A, C, and K and calcium.

Health Benefits

Any type of leafy green, no matter the shade of color, is packed full of vitamins and nutrients. There are small amounts of incomplete protein, which can be especially beneficial in a vegetarian or vegan diet when paired with complementary proteins, such as beans or grains. The cruciferous greens, such as arugula, cabbage, brussels sprouts, watercress, or broccoli raab, are well-known for their cancer fighting and anti-inflammatory properties. The American Cancer Society recommends eating about 2½ cups of vegetables with vibrant colors, such as chard, kale, or radicchio, each day. In addition to being packed with vitamins and minerals, leafy greens are fiber rich and low in calories, so they may help to control your weight.

While not every green will become a favorite, they are all worth trying. Many of the recipes in this book offer leafy green alternatives, as many flavor combinations complement several varieties of greens. All of the health benefits, the ease of preparation, and the affordability of greens will make you want to add them to every meal!

Salads and
Soups

Arugula Salad with Strawberry Balsamic Vinaigrette

A bright and summery salad! You can use walnuts, pistachios, or almonds in place of the pecans.

Serves 2

Vinaigrette:

1 cup sliced strawberries

3 tablespoons balsamic vinegar

3 tablespoons olive oil

1 teaspoon Dijon mustard

1 teaspoon honey

⅛ teaspoon salt, or to taste

Salad:

3 cups packed arugula

¼ cup toasted pecans, divided

1 ounce crumbled goat cheese

¼ cup mandarin orange segments

In a food processor or blender, pulse all the ingredients for the vinaigrette until well mixed and uniform in color.

In a large bowl, toss the arugula and half of the pecans with the desired amount of vinaigrette. If any vinaigrette is left over, it can remain in the refrigerator for up to 3 days. Divide the arugula between two plates, and top with the remaining pecans, the goat cheese, and the mandarin orange segments. Serve immediately.

Quinoa, Fennel, and Arugula Salad

Light and fresh tasting, this salad makes a great starter or side dish. You can substitute other grains if quinoa is not available.

Serves 4

Quinoa:

½ cup quinoa

1 cup vegetable broth or water

Pinch of salt

Vinaigrette:

1 cup fresh orange juice (from about 1 large orange or 2 medium oranges)

¼ cup lime juice (from about 1½ limes)

Zest of 1 orange and 1 lime

1 small shallot, minced

¼ cup olive oil

¼ cup apple cider vinegar

Dash of hot sauce, such as Tabasco

Arugula Salad:

1 fennel bulb, very thinly sliced, fronds reserved

1 (15-ounce) can cannellini beans, drained and rinsed

2 cups packed chopped arugula

1 cup halved cherry tomatoes

Salt and pepper

2 tablespoons shaved Parmesan cheese

In a small pot over medium heat, stir the quinoa into the broth or water and salt, bring to a simmer, and cook until tender, about 20 minutes.

To make the vinaigrette, add the citrus juices and zests, shallot, oil, vinegar, and hot sauce to a food processor or blender. Pulse until emulsified, then set aside.

Assemble the salad by combining the cooked quinoa, sliced fennel, cannellini beans, arugula, tomatoes, and vinaigrette in a large bowl. Season with salt and pepper to taste. Divide among plates and sprinkle with the Parmesan cheese and fennel fronds. This can be stored in the refrigerator, undressed, for up to 3 days.

White Bean Soup with Arugula and Potato

Arugula doesn't have to be relegated to just salads. This soup showcases the peppery green alongside beans and potatoes to make a filling meal for fall or winter. This soup also works well with other spicy greens, such as mustard greens and dandelion greens.

Serves 4

3 tablespoons canola oil

1 small onion, finely diced

1 rib celery, finely diced

1 large carrot, finely diced

3 cloves garlic, minced

8 cups (2 quarts) chicken or vegetable broth, or water

1 pound Yukon Gold potatoes, peeled and finely diced

1 bay leaf

2 cups packed arugula

1 (15-ounce) can cannellini beans, drained and rinsed

Salt and pepper

½ cup shaved Parmesan cheese

In a 6-quart stockpot over medium heat, warm the oil until it shimmers. Add the onion, celery, and carrot, and cook until the onion becomes translucent, 2 to 3 minutes, stirring occasionally. Add the garlic, stirring constantly, for about 1 minute, until fragrant. Add the broth or water, potato, and bay leaf. Simmer for 10 minutes, covered, until the potato is fork tender. Stir in the arugula. Using an immersion or stick blender, puree half of the soup, leaving some pieces of potato whole. Add the beans, cover, and allow the soup to simmer for an additional 5 to 10 minutes. Season with salt and pepper to taste. Ladle into serving bowls and top with Parmesan cheese. This soup can be cooled, covered, and stored in the refrigerator for up to 5 days.

Bibb or Butterhead Lettuce Wraps with Tamarind Sauce

Quick and fresh, this is an ideal meal for summer and requires only a small amount of preparation. You can use pork or beef instead of chicken and add other vegetables if you'd like. The filling and sauce may be made 1 day ahead and stored, covered, in the refrigerator.

Serves 4

Garlic Ginger Chicken:

1 tablespoon sesame oil

1 pound chicken cutlets, sliced into ½-inch strips

3 cloves garlic, minced

½ inch fresh ginger, grated

2 tablespoons soy sauce

Dash of black pepper

1 teaspoon sesame seeds

Tamarind Sauce:

1 tablespoon tamarind paste

½ cup hot water

2 tablespoons sugar

1 tablespoon chili garlic sauce

1 teaspoon soy sauce

¼ teaspoon fish sauce

Lettuce Wraps and Filling:

12 large Bibb or butterhead lettuce leaves

2 cups cooked bean thread noodles

1 medium carrot, shredded

1 medium red bell pepper, cut into matchsticks

½ cup bean sprouts

½ cup packed cilantro

2 scallions, green parts only, thinly sliced

In a medium skillet over medium heat, warm the sesame oil until it shimmers. Add the chicken strips and cook until opaque, about 2 minutes. Add the garlic and ginger and cook, stirring, for 30 seconds. Combine the soy sauce, pepper, and sesame seeds in a small bowl, then pour over the chicken, bring to a simmer for 1 to 2 minutes, until cooked through, and remove from the heat.

In a small bowl, whisk together the tamarind paste, hot water, sugar, chili garlic sauce, soy sauce, and fish sauce until well combined. Set aside to cool.

Divide the ingredients among four plates, stacking the lettuce leaves, noodles, cooked chicken, carrot, bell pepper, and sprouts, arranging them in piles around the plates. Garnish the plates with cilantro. Divide the sauce into 4 small bowls, sprinkle with scallions and serve alongside the wraps. The filling and sauce may be made 1 day ahead and stored, covered, in the refrigerator.

Bok Choy Soup with Tofu

This soup has a lot of different textures, with the slight crunch of the bok choy, the firmness of the shiitake mushrooms, and the silkiness of the tofu. This recipe has a very mild flavor, but you could add some spice with the addition of chili oil.

Serves 4

1 cup dried shiitake mushrooms

2 cups hot water

1 tablespoon sesame oil

1 small onion, finely diced

3 cloves garlic, minced

1 tablespoon minced fresh ginger

1 cup diced carrot

12 cups (3 quarts) mushroom or vegetable broth

½ cup soy sauce

1 tablespoon mirin

1 (14-ounce) block firm or extra-firm tofu, drained and diced

4 cups packed chopped bok choy

½ cup chopped scallion, both white and green parts

Black pepper

Rehydrate the mushrooms in the hot water for 10 minutes. In a 6-quart stockpot over medium heat, warm the oil until it shimmers. Cook the onion until translucent, 2 to 3 minutes, stirring occasionally. Add the garlic, ginger, and carrot, cooking for 30 seconds, and then add the rehydrated mushrooms along with the water in which they soaked. Pour in the broth, soy sauce, and mirin. Bring to a boil, reduce the heat to medium-low, and add the tofu. Allow to simmer for 10 minutes, covered. Add the bok choy and simmer for an additional 5 minutes, until the stems begin to soften. Stir in the green onion, and season with pepper to taste. This soup can be cooled, covered, and stored in the refrigerator for up to 5 days.

Bok Choy Salad with Ginger Sesame Dressing and Sesame Chicken

Fresh and filling, this salad gets dressed up with the savory, sweet, and zesty dressing. You can make this vegetarian by marinating and searing tofu or tempeh instead of chicken.

Serves 4

Sesame Chicken:

2 tablespoons minced fresh ginger

3 tablespoons sesame oil

¼ cup soy sauce

3 tablespoons rice vinegar

1 pound boneless, skinless chicken breasts

Dressing:

1 tablespoons fresh orange juice

1 tablespoons sesame oil

¾ tablespoons soy sauce

¾ tablespoons rice vinegar

1 teaspoon minced fresh ginger

1 clove garlic

½ teaspoon brown sugar

½ teaspoon chili sauce

Salad:

4 cups bok choy, sliced in ½-inch strips

3 medium carrots, sliced into ribbons with a vegetable peeler

¼ cup slivered almonds

1 tablespoon sesame seeds

1 cup cooked white or brown rice

2 scallions, green parts only, thinly sliced, for garnish (optional)

To make the sesame chicken marinade, combine the ginger, sesame oil, soy sauce, and rice vinegar in a resealable bag. Add the chicken and refrigerate for 20 minutes to marinate. Heat a medium skillet over medium heat. Remove the chicken from the marinade, reserving the marinade, and cook 2 to 3 minutes on each side. Add the marinade and enough water to cover the chicken. Cover, reduce the heat to low, and simmer until the chicken is cooked through, about 20 minutes. Allow the cooked chicken to cool. Once cooled, thinly slice the chicken or shred it with a fork.

Prepare the dressing by placing the orange juice, sesame oil, soy sauce, rice vinegar, ginger, garlic, brown sugar, and chili sauce in a food processor. Pulse until the ingredients are well blended.

In a large bowl, combine the bok choy, carrots, almonds, sesame seeds, rice, and ginger sesame dressing. Mix until the dressing coats all the salad ingredients. Divide the salad among four plates and top with sliced chicken and garnish with green onion, if using.

Chard Panzanella

Panzanella is an Italian salad made with bread and tomatoes. This version gets a kick of color and flavor by adding chard.

Serves 6

¾ cup extra-virgin olive oil, divided

3 large slices crusty bread, such as ciabatta

Pinch of salt

Pinch of pepper

2 cups halved cherry tomatoes

¼ cup basil leaves, chopped

3 cups loosely packed de-stemmed, chopped Swiss chard leaves

4 tablespoons balsamic vinegar, divided

2 cloves garlic, minced

1 tablespoon agave nectar

Preheat a grill or medium skillet over medium heat. Brush 2 tablespoons of the olive oil onto the bread and sprinkle with salt and pepper. Grill the bread, turning once, until lightly charred on each side. Remove and let cool. Once cooled, slice into 1-inch cubes.

Mix together the cherry tomatoes, basil, and Swiss chard. In a small bowl, whisk together 2 tablespoons more olive oil, 2 tablespoons of the balsamic vinegar, and the garlic and agave. Add the dressing to the chard Swiss chard mixture and massage it into the leaves to gently bruise the leaves and evenly coat them with dressing. Add the remaining 6 tablespoons olive oil and 2 tablespoons balsamic vinegar, add the charred bread cubes, and gently toss together. Allow the salad to sit for 10 minutes before serving, so the bread can absorb a small amount of dressing, but don't let it get soggy. The salad is best eaten within 2 hours.

Endive and Apple Salad

The endive mellows with this acidic dressing and the sweetness of the apples.

Serves 4

Dressing:

2 tablespoons olive oil

1 tablespoons apple cider
  vinegar

½ tablespoon orange juice

½ teaspoon honey

Dash of salt

Salad:

¼ cup unsalted pecans

2 small heads Belgian endive,
  chopped

1 cup packed arugula

1 medium Granny Smith
  apple, thinly sliced

¼ dried cherries or
  cranberries

1 ounce crumbled goat
  cheese (optional)

To make the dressing, whisk together the oil, vinegar, juice, and honey in a small bowl. Season with salt.

In a small dry sauté pan over medium heat, toast the pecans, stirring constantly, until they're fragrant, 6 to 8 minutes. Remove from the heat and let cool.

Mix together the endive, arugula, apple, and cherries or cranberries in a medium bowl. Toss with the dressing. Top with the toasted pecans and goat cheese, if using.

Escarole Soup

The bitterness of escarole mellows as it cooks in this comforting soup filled with chunks of chicken. Make this vegetarian by using vegetable broth and substituting tempeh for the chicken.

Serves 4

2 tablespoons olive oil

1 medium onion, diced

3 cloves garlic, minced

2 medium carrots, diced

2 ribs celery, finely diced

12 cups (3 quarts) chicken broth or water

½ teaspoon dried thyme

½ teaspoon dried oregano

1 tablespoon dried parsley

1½ pounds boneless, skinless chicken breast, diced into 1-inch cubes

3 cups packed chopped escarole

Salt and pepper

¼ cup shaved Parmesan cheese

In a 6-quart stockpot over medium heat, warm the oil until it shimmers. Sauté the onion until it starts to become translucent, about 2 minutes. Add the garlic, carrot, and celery, cooking until soft, about 2 minutes. Add the broth or water, cover, and bring to a boil. Stir in the thyme, oregano, parsley, and diced chicken, reduce the heat to low, and simmer for 5 to 10 minutes covered, or until the chicken is cooked through. Add the escarole, stir, and season with salt and pepper to taste. Ladle into serving bowls and top with the Parmesan cheese. This soup can be cooled, covered, and stored in the refrigerator for up to 5 days.

Black Bean, Corn, and Kale Salad

Make this salad for an easy meal, or bring it along to picnics or barbecues since it travels so well! You can make this a heartier meal by adding rice or other grains.

Serves 6

1 (15-ounce) can black beans, drained and rinsed

1 (15-ounce) can corn, drained and rinsed

2 cups packed de-stemmed, chopped kale

1 cup halved cherry tomatoes

1 jalapeño chile pepper, seeded and minced

¼ cup fresh lime juice

2 tablespoons extra-virgin olive oil

2 tablespoons chopped cilantro

Salt and pepper

Place the black beans and corn in a large bowl. Add the kale, tomatoes, and jalapeño to the bean and corn mixture.

In a small bowl, combine the lime juice, olive oil, and cilantro. Whisk and pour over the salad, stirring until all the ingredients are lightly dressed. Season with salt and pepper to taste. This is best eaten within 2 hours of dressing.

Kale Salad with Avocado

Packed full of vitamin C and heart-healthy monounsaturated fat, this salad is easy to prepare.

Serves 4

Juice of 1 lemon (about ¼ cup)

¼ cup olive oil

4 cups packed de-stemmed, chopped kale

½ cup slivered almonds

1 ripe avocado, diced

1 cup halved cherry tomatoes

Salt and pepper

In a small bowl, whisk together the lemon juice, olive oil, and salt and pepper to taste. Massage the dressing on the kale, and top with the almonds, avocado, and cherry tomatoes. Serve within 1 hour of cutting the avocado and adding the dressing.

Kale Salad with Butternut Squash, Cranberries, and Pepitas

This colorful salad combines some of the flavors of autumn and uses pepitas, also known as pumpkin seeds. Feel free to use chard instead of kale and to experiment with other squash, such as delicata or pumpkin.

Serves 4

Roasted Squash:

1 pound butternut squash
2 tablespoons olive oil
Pinch of salt
Pinch of pepper

Kale Salad:

¼ cup apple cider
2 tablespoons apple cider vinegar
2 tablespoons olive oil
1 tablespoon maple syrup
Salt and pepper
6 to 8 cups packed de-stemmed, chopped kale
½ cup dried cranberries

Pepita Topping:

1 tablespoon olive oil
½ cup pepitas
⅛ teaspoon ground cinnamon
1 teaspoon brown sugar
Dash of salt

Preheat the oven to 400°F. Peel the squash, cut in half, and scoop out the seeds. Cut the squash into ½-inch half-moons. Toss the squash with the oil, salt, and pepper. Place in a single layer on a baking sheet and roast for 20 minutes, turning the squash after 10 minutes. Remove from the oven and let cool.

In a small bowl, mix together the apple cider, cider vinegar, olive oil, maple syrup, and salt and pepper to taste. Drizzle a little of the dressing at a time over the kale and gently rub the dressing over the leaves to coat. Toss the kale with the cranberries.

In a separate small bowl, mix together the olive oil, pepitas, cinnamon, brown sugar, and salt. Toast the pepitas in a shallow pan over low heat, just until they start to puff up and become fragrant, 6 to 8 minutes. Set aside to cool.

Divide the squash on plates, then top with equal amounts of the kale and the toasted pepitas.

Kale Soup with Sausage and Potatoes

A filling soup, this is quick and easy comfort food. It can be made vegetarian by substituting tempeh or tofu for the sausage and by adding ¼ teaspoon fennel seeds. Serve it with crusty bread or a fresh salad, if desired.

Serves 6

3 tablespoons canola oil, divided

2 cooked Italian sausages, sliced into ¼-inch medallions

1 small onion, finely diced

3 small carrots, finely diced

2 ribs celery, finely diced

3 cloves garlic, minced

2 tablespoons tomato paste

8 cups (2 quarts) water

1 pound Yukon Gold potatoes, peeled and finely diced

4 cups packed de-stemmed, chopped kale

1 tablespoon Worcestershire sauce

2 teaspoons red pepper flakes

Salt and pepper

In a 6-quart stockpot, heat 1 tablespoon of the oil over medium heat and sear the sausage until browned. Remove the sausage from the pot and heat the remaining 2 tablespoons oil. Add the onion, carrot, and celery, and cook until the onion becomes translucent, about 2 minutes. Stir in the garlic and tomato paste. Add the water and potatoes. Bring to a boil, reduce the heat to low, cover, and simmer for 10 minutes. Add the kale, seared sausage, Worcestershire sauce, and red pepper flakes. Allow to simmer for an additional 10 to 15 minutes. Season with salt and pepper to taste. This soup can be cooled, covered, and stored in the refrigerator for up to 5 days.

Kale Tabbouleh

This salad makes a light lunch served on its own, or it can be accompanied by pita chips and hummus.

Serves 4

½ cup bulgur wheat

1 cup water

3 cups de-stemmed, packed chopped kale

Juice of 1 small lemon (about 3 tablespoons)

2 tablespoons extra-virgin olive oil

1 cup diced cucumber

1 cup halved cherry tomatoes

2 cloves garlic, minced

Salt and pepper

In a small pot, combine the bulgur and water. Simmer over medium heat until the bulgur is cooked, 5 to 10 minutes. Allow to cool to room temperature.

Massage the lemon juice and olive oil into the kale. Stir in the cucumber, tomatoes, garlic, and cooked bulgur. Season with salt and pepper to taste. Store in the refrigerator for up to 3 days.

Kimchi

This is a Korean side dish or condiment that is fermented and spicy from a fermented red pepper paste called gochujang. It can be served with noodles, alongside meats, or in soups. If you can't find gochujang, you can substitute an equal amount of Sriracha mixed with 2 tablespoons of fish sauce.

Makes 2 quarts

1 small head napa cabbage

1 cup coarse salt

½ cup rice vinegar

1 tablespoon sugar

2 tablespoons gochujang (Korean chili paste)

3 tablespoons red pepper flakes

1 teaspoon fish sauce

1 teaspoon grated fresh ginger

2 scallions, both white and green parts, trimmed and sliced in half

6 cloves garlic, thinly sliced

1 small onion, diced

1 cup quartered and thinly sliced daikon radish

Cut the cabbage into quarters. Remove the tough inner core. Thoroughly wash the cabbage to remove all the dirt. Fill a large bowl or tub with water and add the cabbage. Sprinkle the salt on top. Allow the cabbage to sit for at least 45 minutes or up to 4 hours, then rotate each piece and let sit for an additional 45 minutes, or until wilted. Drain the salted water and replace with fresh water, swishing the cabbage around to remove the salt. Repeat the rinse 2 more times to remove all the salt. Drain the cabbage and slice into smaller pieces, if desired.

In a large bowl, mix together the vinegar, sugar, chili paste, red pepper flakes, and fish sauce. Working in three batches, add a third of the cabbage and a third of the other vegetables to the chile paste mixture. Massage the paste into the vegetables, coating them evenly. Shake off any excess paste and place in desired pickling containers. Continue with the remaining vegetable batches, until they are all coated with chili paste and in pickling containers.

Close the lid(s) tightly and allow to sit, refrigerated, for at least 1 day before enjoying. For a stronger flavor, allow kimchi to sit for up to 2 weeks, shaking occasionally, before enjoying.

Mustard Greens Soup with Ginger

Light and clean-flavored, this soup is best in the late spring or summer. You can make it vegetarian by using vegetable broth in place of chicken broth and replacing the chicken with tofu.

Serves 4

1 tablespoon olive oil

1 small onion, finely chopped

2 cloves garlic, minced

1 tablespoon minced fresh ginger

½ teaspoon red pepper flakes

8 cups (2 quarts) chicken broth or water

1 pound boneless, skinless chicken breasts, diced into 1-inch cubes

1 stalk fresh lemongrass, or 2 (3-inch) pieces dried

3 cups packed de-stemmed, chopped mustard greens

3 scallions, green parts only, diced

¼ cup soy sauce

Black pepper

In a 6-quart stockpot over medium heat, warm the oil until it shimmers. Add the onion and cook until it becomes translucent, 2 to 3 minutes, stirring occasionally. Add the garlic, ginger, and red pepper flakes, and cook, stirring, until fragrant, about 1 minute. Pour in the broth or water and heat to a boil. Stir in the chicken. Bruise the lemongrass by pounding it with a meat-tenderizing hammer, then add it to the soup. Cover, reduce the heat to medium-low, and allow the soup to simmer for 10 to 15 minutes, or until the chicken is cooked through. Using a ladle, remove and discard any foam that may have bubbled to the top. Add the mustard greens, scallions, and soy sauce. Season with black pepper to taste. This soup can be cooled, covered, and stored in the refrigerator for up to 5 days.

Dijon Mustard Greens Salad with Capers and Eggs

Mustard greens, which are usually cooked, are the star in this raw salad. Their flavor mellows out when gently bruised and dressed with the Dijon vinaigrette.

Serves 4

4 large eggs
¼ cup olive oil
¼ cup apple cider vinegar
1 tablespoon Dijon mustard
Salt and pepper
6 cups packed de-stemmed, chopped mustard greens
1 cup thinly sliced red onion
2 tablespoons capers

Place the eggs in a pot and cover with cold water. Bring the water to a boil and then turn off the heat. Allow the eggs to sit in the hot water for 10 minutes before draining them. Shock the eggs by covering them with cold water and adding ice cubes. Peel the eggs and set aside.

In a small bowl, whisk together the oil, vinegar, mustard, and salt and pepper to taste. Pour half of the dressing over the mustard greens. Massage the greens, bruising the leaves gently with your fingers. Add additional dressing, if desired. Divide the greens among four serving dishes. Cut the eggs into quarters and place four quarters on each salad. Divide the onions and capers among the salads. Season with additional salt and pepper to taste. This salad is best consumed within 1 hour of dressing.

Napa Cabbage with Soy Sesame Dressing and Peanuts

This salad can be made with other crisp lettuces such as romaine. Try serving it with coconut shrimp, lemongrass chicken, or spicy beef.

Serves 4

4 cups packed thinly chopped napa cabbage

4 scallions, green parts only, thinly sliced

1 medium carrot, shredded

1 medium red bell pepper, cut into matchsticks

1 jalapeño chile pepper, seeded and minced

¼ cup packed chopped cilantro

2 tablespoons soy sauce

2 tablespoons hot water

1 tablespoon sesame oil

1 tablespoon fresh lime juice

1 tablespoon creamy peanut butter

1 clove garlic, minced

½ cup chopped unsalted peanuts

In a large bowl, combine the cabbage, scallions, carrot, bell pepper, jalapeño, and cilantro. In a small bowl, whisk together the soy sauce, water, sesame oil, lime juice, peanut butter, and garlic. Massage the dressing into the cabbage mixture. Divide among plates, top with the peanuts, and serve.

Once dressed, the salad should be enjoyed the same day. If not dressed, the salad may be kept in the refrigerator for up to 3 days.

Sesame Noodles with Napa Cabbage

Soba noodles are a popular in Japan, where they're often served chilled with a dipping sauce on hot days. In this dish, these noodles get dressed up with cabbage and other vegetables.

Serves 4

2 cups finely chopped napa cabbage

4 scallions, green parts only, thinly sliced

1 small red bell pepper, cut into matchsticks

¼ cup sesame oil

2 tablespoons soy sauce

1 tablespoon rice vinegar

2 tablespoons fresh lime juice (from about 1 lime)

1 tablespoon sugar

½ teaspoon red pepper flakes

2 cups cooked soba noodles

2 tablespoons sesame seeds

In a large bowl, combine the cabbage, scallions, and bell pepper. Whisk together the sesame oil, soy sauce, rice vinegar, lime juice, sugar, and red pepper flakes. Massage the dressing into cabbage, until well combined. Toss with the noodles and divide among plates. Top with the sesame seeds. Once dressed, the cabbage will begin to wilt and should be eaten within a few hours. Without the dressing, the salad can be stored in the refrigerator for up to 3 days.

Southwestern Coleslaw

Coleslaw is traditionally made with green cabbage and mayonnaise. This version is more vibrant in color and flavor, as well as being lower in fat. It makes a great addition to a picnic or barbecue.

Serves 6

6 cups packed thinly sliced red cabbage

1 medium red bell pepper, cut into matchsticks

½ cup packed cilantro, chopped, divided

2 cloves garlic

¼ teaspoon ground cumin

¼ cup fresh lime juice (from about 1½ limes)

½ cup apple cider vinegar

½ cup extra -virgin olive oil

1 tablespoon honey

1 teaspoon hot sauce, such as Tabasco

Salt and pepper

In a large bowl, combine the cabbage, bell pepper, and ¼ cup cilantro. In a blender, combine the remaining ¼ cup cilantro and the garlic, cumin, lime juice, vinegar, olive oil, honey, and hot sauce . Blend until well combined. Toss the cabbage mixture with the dressing until well coated. Season with salt and pepper to taste. This dish can be made 1 day ahead and stored in the refrigerator for up to 5 days, undressed.

Caesar Salad

This dressing is lighter in calories than a traditional Caesar dressing, but you can make it creamier by substituting 1 tablespoon mayonnaise in place of the egg yolk.

Serves 6

Croutons:
1 tablespoon olive oil
1 clove garlic, minced
Dash of chili powder
Salt and pepper
1½ cups cubed bread

Dressing:
2 cloves garlic
2 teaspoons Dijon mustard
1 tablespoon Worcestershire sauce
1 teaspoon red wine vinegar
1 egg yolk
½ teaspoon pepper
Salt

Salad:
1 large head romaine
½ cup shaved Parmesan cheese, divided

Preheat the oven to 350°F. In a small bowl, whisk together the olive oil, garlic, chili powder, and salt and pepper to taste. Gently toss the bread cubes with the seasoned oil. Spread the coated bread cubes in a single layer on a baking sheet and toast in the oven for 10 minutes, or until the desired crispness is reached. Remove from the oven and allow to cool.

To make the dressing, combine the garlic, mustard, Worcestershire sauce, vinegar, egg yolk, and pepper in a food processor or blender. Blend until all of the ingredients are well incorporated. Season with salt to taste.

Cut the romaine in half lengthwise, then cut into 1-inch-wide sections. In a large bowl, toss the romaine with the dressing, croutons, and about a quarter of the Parmesan shavings. Divide among serving plates, and garnish with the remaining Parmesan. The dressing may be made 1 day in advance.

African Peanut Stew

This is a vegetarian stew with big chunks of sweet potato along with tomato and peanut butter as the main ingredients, but you can create your own version by varying the quantities. For a non-vegetarian version of this stew, add chicken legs or thighs. Just season the chicken with salt and pepper, then add it when you add the sweet potato.

Serves 4

1 tablespoon olive oil

1 cup finely diced onion

3 cloves garlic, minced

2 tablespoons minced fresh ginger

1 habanero chile pepper, seeded and minced

4 cups (1 quart) vegetable broth or water

1 (15-ounce) can crushed tomatoes

1 large carrot, diced into ½-inch cubes

1 medium sweet potato, peeled and diced into 1-inch cubes

¼ cup creamy peanut butter

½ teaspoon ground coriander

¼ teaspoon cayenne pepper

2 cups packed chopped spinach or packed de-stemmed, chopped kale

¼ cup packed chopped cilantro

Salt and pepper

¼ cup chopped unsalted peanuts

In a 6-quart stockpot over medium heat, warm the oil until it shimmers. Cook the onion until translucent, about 3 minutes. Add the garlic, ginger, and habanero chile pepper, cooking for another 30 seconds. Add the broth or water, tomatoes, carrot, sweet potato, and peanut butter. Cover, reduce the heat to medium-low, and allow to simmer for 10 minutes, or until the sweet potato is tender. Stir in the coriander, cayenne, spinach or kale, and cilantro. Simmer for an additional 3 minutes, until the spinach or kale is wilted, then season with salt and pepper to taste. Serve hot over rice or another grain. Top each serving with chopped peanuts. This stew can be cooled, covered, and stored in the refrigerator for up to 5 days.

Callaloo (Crab and Greens Soup)

This well-known Caribbean dish, whose texture and ingredients vary by region, originated in West Africa. In some areas, it's pureed and eaten as a soup or sauce, in others it has meat and is reduced to a chunky stew. Callaloo refers to the greens used, often taro (also called dasheen) leaves or amaranth leaves. In North America, spinach—similar in taste and texture to the more traditional greens—is used.

Serves 4

1 tablespoon canola oil

1 cup finely diced onion

4 blue or Dungeness crabs

3 cloves garlic, minced

1 habanero chile pepper, halved and seeded

1 (15-ounce) can coconut milk

4 cups (1 quart) chicken broth or water

3 sprigs fresh thyme or 1 teaspoon dried thyme

4 green onion, both white and green parts, sliced

2 cups pumpkin or sweet potato, peeled and diced into 1-inch cubes

4 cups packed fresh spinach

Salt and pepper

In a 6-quart stockpot over medium heat, warm the oil until it shimmers. Sauté the onion until translucent, 2 to 4 minutes. Place the rinsed crabs in the pot and add the garlic, habanero chile pepper, coconut milk, and broth. Cover, bring to boil, then reduce the heat to low and simmer until the crabs turn red and are cooked, about 5 minutes. Remove the crabs and the chile pepper halves, then add the thyme, green onion, and pumpkin or sweet potato. Simmer until the pumpkin or sweet potato is tender, 8 to 10 minutes.

Using a stick or immersion blender, puree half of the soup, leaving some of it chunky. Remove the crabmeat from the shells. Add the meat and the spinach, season with salt and pepper to taste, and simmer until the spinach has wilted, about 2 minutes. This soup can be cooled, covered, and stored in the refrigerator for up to 3 days.

Watercress and Potato Soup

This soup is peppery and fresh tasting. You can use both the stems and leaves in this recipe, so there is very little waste.

Serves 4

2 tablespoons olive oil

1 medium onion, diced

4 cloves garlic, minced

2 ribs celery, finely diced

½ teaspoon dried thyme

8 cups (2 quarts) chicken or vegetable broth

3 large Yukon Gold potatoes, peeled and diced

6 cups packed chopped watercress

½ cup heavy cream

1 tablespoon fresh lemon juice

Salt and pepper

¼ cup scallions or chives, for garnish (optional)

½ cup grated Parmesan cheese, for garnish (optional)

In a 6-quart stockpot over medium heat, warm the oil until it shimmers. Cook the onion until it becomes translucent, about 2 minutes. Add the garlic, celery, and thyme, cooking until soft, about 2 minutes. Add the broth or water, cover, and bring to a boil, then reduce the heat to low, and bring to a simmer. Add the potato and simmer for 5 to 10 minutes, or until the potato becomes tender. Stir in the watercress, and then stir in the heavy cream and then the lemon juice. Season with salt and pepper to taste. Ladle into serving bowls and top with scallions or chives and Parmesan cheese, if desired. This soup can be cooled, covered, and stored in the refrigerator for up to 5 days.

Chilled Watercress Soup

On those days when it is too hot to even think about cooking, you can throw together this soup and enjoy a cool and refreshing meal.

Serves 4

½ medium cucumber, peeled and diced

4 cups packed watercress

2 cups frozen peas

3 cups chicken or vegetable broth

¼ cup plain yogurt

3 tablespoons balsamic vinegar

Salt and pepper

¼ cup crumbled feta or goat cheese (optional)

Add the cucumber, watercress, peas, broth, yogurt, and balsamic vinegar to a blender, and blend until smooth. Season with salt and pepper to taste. Pour into serving bowls and top with feta or goat cheese, if desired. This can be made ahead and stored covered in the refrigerator for up to 3 days.

Appetizers,
Snacks, **and**
Side **Dishes**

Arugula Hummus

A traditional hummus with the added flavor and nutrition of arugula, this can be an appetizer or snack with sliced vegetables and pita, or spread on to sandwiches.

Makes about 2 cups

1 (15-ounce) can chickpeas, drained and rinsed

1 clove garlic

1 cup packed arugula

3 tablespoons fresh lemon juice

1 tablespoon tahini

¼ cup olive oil

¼ cup water, or as needed

Salt

In a blender or food processor, combine the chickpeas, garlic, arugula, lemon juice, tahini, and olive oil. Blend or pulse until smooth. Add water 1 tablespoon at a time if a smoother texture is desired. Season with salt to taste.

Arugula Pesto

Pesto is usually made with basil, but spicy arugula works perfectly in its place. You can use this on bruschetta, tossed with pasta, or on top of chicken.

Makes ½ cup

2 cups packed arugula

1 tablespoon pine nuts

1 clove garlic

¼ cup grated Parmesan cheese

¼ cup olive oil

2 tablespoons fresh lemon juice

Salt and pepper

Place all the ingredients in the bowl of a food processor, and pulse until well blended.

Chimichurri

This Argentinean sauce may be used as a marinade for meats or as a sauce for veggies or pasta. If you're not a fan of cilantro, it may be omitted.

Makes 1 cup

1 cup packed parsley
⅓ cup olive oil
2 tablespoons chopped cilantro
2 tablespoons fresh oregano
3 cloves garlic
1 tablespoon red wine vinegar
1 tablespoon fresh lemon juice
¼ teaspoon red pepper flakes
Salt, to taste

Place all the ingredients in the bowl of a food processor, and pulse until well blended. Season with salt to taste.

Barley with Beet, Arugula, and Goat Cheese

This makes a beautiful side dish but is hearty enough to be served alone. If you use red beets, this dish will turn a bright shade of magenta, but not when made with golden beets. This can be made with other greens, like spinach, kale, or chard.

Serves 4

1 small beet, any variety
2 tablespoons olive oil
½ small onion, finely diced
1 clove garlic, minced
1 cup pearled barley
2 cups chicken or vegetable broth, or water
1 cup packed arugula
Salt and pepper
¼ cup crumbled goat cheese

Preheat the oven to 400°F. Wrap the beet in aluminum foil and bake in the oven for 40 minutes, or until easily pierced with a knife. Allow to cool slightly. Peel the beet by placing it in a paper towel and rubbing off the skin. Dice into ½-inch pieces.

In a medium pot over medium heat, warm the oil until it shimmers. Add the onion and cook until translucent, 2 to 3 minutes. Add the garlic and cook for 1 minute, stirring occasionally. Stir in the barley and the broth or water. Cover, reduce the heat to medium-low, and simmer for 20 minutes, or until the barley is cooked and tender. Stir in the arugula and gently fold in the diced beet. Season with salt and pepper to taste. Divide among the serving plates and top with crumbled goat cheese.

Beet Greens with Fruits and Nuts

These colorful greens are full of vitamins and are often overlooked in the produce department, which keeps them affordable. This is a sweet way of cooking them and a kid-friendly recipe.

Serves 4

8 cups water

4 cups packed beet greens (about 1 bunch)

2 tablespoons olive oil

½ small sweet onion, finely diced

½ cup dried mixed fruits, such as apricots, cranberries, cherries, and pears

1 cup Granny Smith apple, finely diced (about ½ medium apple)

½ cup toasted chopped nuts, such as almonds, walnuts, or pecans

1 tablespoon sherry vinegar

Boil the water in a 4-quart pot over medium-high heat. Blanch the beet greens by placing them into the boiling water until wilted, 30 seconds to 1 minute, then shocking them, or stopping the cooking process, by plunging them into a bowl of ice water. After shocking them, drain the greens then gently squeeze out the water. Chop the blanched beet greens into ribbons.

In a small dry sauté pan over medium heat, toast the nuts until they begin to smell buttery and toasty, then remove them and let them cool. In a large pan over medium-low heat, warm the oil until it shimmers, then add the onion and mixed fruits. Cook, stirring occasionally, until the onion becomes translucent, about 2 minutes. Add the blanched beet greens and cook for an additional 2 or 3 minutes. Stir in the toasted nuts and the vinegar.

Warm Citrus Beet Greens

Beet greens brighten up with a bit of citrus. You can use dandelion greens if beet greens aren't available.

Serves 4

1 large beet, any variety

2 tablespoons olive oil

1 clove garlic, minced

1 bunch beet greens, de-stemmed and sliced into 3-inch pieces

¼ cup fresh orange juice

Salt and pepper

Preheat the oven to 400°F. Wrap the beet in aluminum foil and bake in the oven for 40 minutes, or until easily pierced with a knife. Allow to cool slightly. Peel the beet by placing it in a paper towel and rubbing off the skin. Dice into ½-inch pieces.

When the beet is done, heat the oil in a large skillet over medium heat. Cook the garlic for 1 to 2 minutes, until fragrant, stirring occasionally. Add the greens and orange juice, stirring occasionally, until the greens have wilted, about 2 minutes. Season with salt and pepper to taste. Slice the beet into thin rounds and toss with the greens.

Brussels Sprouts with Bacon and Cherries

Bacon goes so well with brussels sprouts and the sweetness of cherries. Cooking the bacon on low heat renders the fat, giving you a flavorful base to cook the brussels sprouts. If you'd like to lower the saturated fat, you can cook with 2 tablespons olive oil instead.

Serves 4 to 6

4 cups brussels sprouts

2 tablespoons dried cherries or cranberries

¼ cup hot water

4 slices bacon

1 medium shallot, minced

Salt and pepper

Trim off the bottoms and remove the outer leaves of the brussels sprouts. Slice very thinly using a mandoline.

In a small bowl, rehydrate the cherries or cranberries in the hot water for 10 minutes.

In a medium skillet over low heat, cook the bacon until crisp, 10 to 15 minutes, turning to avoid burning. Once crisp, remove the bacon, drain on paper towels, and let cool.

Drain most of the bacon fat from the pan, leaving about 2 tablespoons, and turn the heat to medium. Add the shallot and cook until it begins to brown, about 2 minutes. Add the brussels sprouts and cook, stirring occasionally, until the leaves begin to wilt, about 3 minutes. Add the rehydrated cherries or cranberries along with the water in which they soaked. Simmer for an additional 2 minutes. Season with salt and pepper to taste. Dice the crisped bacon into small pieces and sprinkle on top.

Bok Choy Adobo

A well-known dish of the Philippines, adobo gets its flavors from soy sauce, vinegar, and black peppercorns. While simple, this dish is very flavorful. Filipina wives often claim it was their adobo that made their husbands fall in love with them.

Serves 4

1 tablespoon olive oil

2 cloves garlic, minced

1 teaspoon fresh ginger, minced

4 cups packed chopped bok choy

1 tablespoon rice vinegar

2 tablespoons soy sauce

5 black peppercorns

In a large skillet over medium heat, warm the oil until it shimmers. Cook the garlic and ginger for 30 seconds, or until the edges begin to brown. Add the bok choy, vinegar, soy sauce, and black peppercorns. Cook until the stems of the bok choy have softened. Serve over rice. This can be stored in the refrigerator for up to 5 days.

Pomegranate-Glazed Brussels Sprouts with Toasted Pecans

A great side for Thanksgiving, this dish only takes about 15 minutes to prepare and is kid-friendly. The glaze is a little sweet and tangy, and the pecans offer a nice crunch.

Serves 4

1 cup pomegranate juice
¼ cup balsamic vinegar
1 teaspoon honey
1 tablespoon canola oil
1 small onion, diced
1 pound brussels sprouts, trimmed and quartered
Salt and pepper
¼ cup chopped pecans

In a small pot, simmer the pomegranate juice and balsamic vinegar until it has reduced to ¼ cup. Remove the reduction from the heat and stir in the honey.

In a large sauté pan over medium heat, warm the oil until it shimmers. Add the onion and cook until it begins to become translucent, about 2 minutes. Add the brussels sprouts and cook, stirring often, until they begin to soften and can be pierced with a fork, about 5 minutes.

In a small dry skillet, toast the pecans until they begin to turn golden and smell nutty, about 2 minutes. Remove from the heat. Pour the pomegranate reduction over the cooked brussels sprouts and toss to coat. Season with salt and pepper to taste, and top with the toasted pecans.

Roasted Shaved Brussels Sprouts with Parmesan

With clean flavors that complement most main dishes, this side can be made in only 20 minutes. You can substitute Gruyère for the Parmesan.

Serves 4

¼ cup plus 1 tablespoon olive oil, divided
1 pound brussels sprouts
1 teaspoon Dijon mustard
¼ cup shaved Parmesan cheese
Salt and pepper

Preheat the oven to 400°F. Trim the bottoms of the brussels sprouts. Shave the sprouts with a mandoline, or cut the sprouts in half and slice them very thinly. Place the shaved sprouts in a 9 x 13-inch baking dish and drizzle with ¼ cup of the olive oil. Bake for 8 to 10 minutes, or until the shaved sprouts are tender and start to brown on the edges.

In a medium bowl, whisk together the mustard and the remaining 1 tablespoon olive oil, and toss with the roasted sprouts. Season with salt and pepper to taste. Top each serving with Parmesan cheese.

Colcannon

This traditional Irish dish combines potatoes and cabbage, but it can be made with other greens, such as kale or spinach.

Serves 4

3 pounds Idaho or Yukon Gold potatoes, peeled and diced into 1-inch cubes

4 tablespoons unsalted butter

½ cup milk or heavy cream

3 cups medium-diced green cabbage

1 cup finely diced onion

2 cups water

¼ cup chopped chives (optional)

Salt and pepper

In a large pot of water over medium-high heat, boil the potatoes for 15 to 20 minutes, or until easily pierced with a fork. Drain the potatoes. Mash the potatoes with the butter and milk or cream and return to the pot.

In a large skillet over medium-low heat, add the cabbage and onion. Cover with 2 cups of water and bring to a simmer. Cook until the cabbage is tender, about 15 minutes.

Add the cooked cabbage and onion to the mashed potatoes along with the chives, if using. Season with salt and pepper to taste.

Press plastic wrap firmly on the surface of the potato mixture to prevent a skin from forming. This can be stored in the refrigerator for up to 5 days.

Red Wine–Braised Cabbage and Apples

Tender and sweet, this classic recipe derives richness from the red wine. You can add color—and health boosting phytochemicals—to your meal with this beautiful maroon dish.

Serves 6

1 tablespoon olive oil

1 cup finely diced onion

1 small red cabbage, diced

1 medium Granny Smith apple, cored and cut into 8 wedges

1 tablespoon brown sugar

½ cup red wine, such as Cabernet

1 teaspoon apple cider vinegar

3 cups chicken or vegetable broth, or water

Salt and pepper

In a large stockpot over medium heat, warm the oil until it shimmers. Add the onion and cook until the edges begin to brown, 6 to 8 minutes. Stir in the cabbage, apple, brown sugar, wine, vinegar, and broth or water. Bring to a simmer, cover with a lid, and cook for 45 minutes, or until the cabbage is very tender. Season with salt and pepper. This may be stored in the refrigerator for up to 5 days.

Roasted Cabbage

Roasting cabbage brings out its sweetness. Cutting the raw cabbage into thick, round slices is pretty and helps the cabbage cook evenly. You can use red or green cabbage, but red cabbage turns a dark brown color, which some may find undesirable.

Serves 4

1 medium cabbage head, cut into 1-inch-thick slices

Olive oil, enough to lightly coat

Dash of salt

Dash of pepper

Preheat the oven to 425°F. Place the cabbage slices in a single layer on a baking sheet. Drizzle with olive oil and season with salt and pepper. Roast in the oven for 35 to 45 minutes, or until the cabbage begins to brown. The roasted cabbage can be stored in the refrigerator for up to 5 days.

Vegetable Egg Rolls

These can be an appetizer, a side dish, or easily become a meal on their own. This version is vegetarian, but could be made with ground chicken, pork, or beef. After sautéing the onion and garlic, add the ground meat and cook through before adding the vegetables.

Makes 20 rolls

2 tablespoons olive oil

1 small onion, diced

3 cloves garlic, minced

1 pound shredded green or red cabbage

1 small carrot, shredded

3 tablespoons soy sauce

½ teaspoon sugar

2 teaspoons minced fresh ginger

Black pepper

2 cups canola oil

1 package egg roll wrappers (about 20 wrappers)

1 tablespoon cornstarch

2 tablespoons water

To make the egg roll filling, in a large skillet over medium heat, warm the oil until it shimmers. Add the onion and cook until it starts to become translucent, about 2 minutes. Add the garlic and cook until fragrant, about 1 minute. Add the cabbage, carrot, soy sauce, sugar, and ginger. Cook the mixture until the cabbage has wilted, about 4 minutes. Season with black pepper to taste. Drain any excess liquid and allow to cool enough to handle. The filling can be made 1 day ahead.

To make the egg rolls, in a large pot over medium heat, warm the canola oil to 350°F, using a thermometer to check the temperature. Meanwhile, lay out a wrapper so that a point is facing you, and keep the remaining wrappers covered to prevent them from drying out. Place 1 to 2 tablespoons of the drained cabbage mixture near the bottom point, about ¼ inch away from the edge. Stir the cornstarch and water together. Using your finger or a pastry brush, paint a thin coat of the moistened cornstarch onto the edges of the wrapper. To fold the egg roll, start with the bottom corner and fold it over the cabbage. Next fold the left and the right corners over the cabbage, creating an envelope. Then roll the wrapper tightly from the bottom toward the top, using cornstarch to seal it, if needed. Repeat with the remaining wrappers.

Fry the egg rolls in the hot oil, a few at a time to maintain the proper oil temperature, until lightly browned. Remove with a slotted spoon and drain on paper towels. These can be stored in the refrigerator for up to 5 days and reheated in the oven at 350°F for 10 minutes.

Southern-Style Collards with Red Beans and Rice

This is a classic side dish found in Louisiana. You can make this vegetarian by omitting the bacon, using 2 tablespoons of vegetable oil to cook with, and adding twice as much paprika.

Serves 4

3 slices bacon, cut in half

1 cup finely diced onion

4 cloves garlic, mined

1 cup white or jasmine rice

1 (15-ounce) can diced tomatoes

1 bay leaf

1 teaspoon dried thyme

½ teaspoon cayenne pepper

1 tablespoon paprika

1 teaspoon hot sauce, such as Tabasco

1 tablespoon apple cider vinegar

3 cups packed de-stemmed, finely chopped collards

2 cups chicken broth or water

Salt and pepper

In a medium pot over low heat, cook the bacon until the edges begin to brown, about 10 minutes. Increase the heat to medium, then add the onion and cook until it becomes translucent, about 2 minutes. Add the garlic and rice, and stir to coat with the bacon fat. Add the tomatoes, bay leaf, thyme, cayenne, paprika, hot sauce, vinegar, collards, and broth or water, stirring to combine. Cover, reduce the heat to low, and cook for 20 to 25 minutes, or until the rice is tender. Season with salt and pepper to taste. This can be stored in the refrigerator for up to 5 days.

Spicy Collard Greens

Served year-round in the South, this traditional collard recipe is often served with cornbread, though it is also delicious on its own.

Serves 4

1 tablespoon olive oil
1 small onion, diced
2 cloves garlic, minced
1 ham hock
6 cups packed de-stemmed, chopped collard greens (about 1 large bunch)
1 (15-ounce) can diced tomatoes
2 cups chicken broth or water
1 teaspoon red pepper flakes
Salt and pepper

In a large pot (5 quarts or more) over medium heat, warm the oil until it shimmers. Cook the onion and garlic until the onion becomes translucent, 2 to 3 minutes, stirring occasionally. Add the ham hock, collards, tomatoes, water, and red pepper flakes. Cover, reduce the heat to medium-low, and simmer for 30 minutes, or until the collards are tender. Add more water if the collards become too dry. Season with salt and pepper to taste.

Spicy Sautéed Dandelion Greens

Dandelion greens are best eaten in the spring when the greens are small, tender, and have a mild flavor. The larger and older leaves have a much stronger flavor.

Serves 4

1 tablespoon vegetable oil
2 tablespoons minced garlic
2 cups packed, chopped dandelion greens, in 2-inch strips
1 teaspoon red pepper flakes
Salt and pepper
1 teaspoon sugar (optional)

In a large sauté pan over medium heat, warm the oil until it shimmers. Add the garlic and cook for 30 seconds, stirring. Add the dandelion greens and red pepper flakes, stirring until the greens have wilted, about 3 minutes. Season with salt and pepper to taste. If the greens are too bitter, add the sugar. This dish can be stored, covered, in the refrigerator for up to 5 days.

Endive Bites with Blue Cheese, Pecans, and Berries

Endive is the perfect shape for holding dips and fillings. Here it's paired with sweet summer berries, blue cheese, and a drizzle of honey.

Serves 6

2 heads Belgian endive
¼ cup crumbled blue cheese
¼ cup pecans
¼ cup finely diced fresh strawberries
¼ cup fresh blueberries
¼ cup honey

Trim the bottoms off the endive heads, and separate the leaves, removing any inner leaves which may be too small. Mix together the blue cheese and pecans in a food processor, pulsing only until just combined. In a medium bowl, carefully fold the pecan and cheese mixture with the strawberries and blueberries. Evenly divide the mixture onto the endive leaves and drizzle with honey.

Endive Gratin

This is a twist on a traditional gratin recipe, using Belgian endive instead of potatoes. This works well with rapini, too.

Serves 6

1 cup chicken or vegetable broth
1 cup heavy cream
1 tablespoon all-purpose flour
1¼ cups grated Parmesan or Gruyère cheese, divided
6 heads Belgian endive, cut in half, small center leaves and stem removed
Salt and pepper
¼ cup panko breadcrumbs

Preheat the oven to 350°F. In a small saucepan over medium heat, warm the broth and cream. Whisk in the flour and cook until thickened. Stir in ½ cup cheese. Pour half of the cheese sauce in an even layer onto the bottom of a 9 x 13-inch baking dish. Place the endive leaves in two layers on top of the sauce, sprinkling ¼ cup cheese, salt, and pepper between the top and bottom layers. Top with the remaining sauce, ½ cup cheese and the breadcrumbs. Bake for 30 minutes, or until the cheese has melted and the breadcrumbs are golden brown.

Grilled Endive

Simply grilling endive really accentuates the flavor of this leafy green. You can use this technique for kale and romaine, as well.

Serves 4

4 heads Belgian endive
4 tablespoons olive oil
Dash salt and pepper
¼ cup blue cheese (optional)

Preheat the grill. Cut the endive heads in half lengthwise. Wash thoroughly and pat dry. Brush the endive halves on all sides with the oil, and season with salt and pepper. Grill each side for 1 to 2 minutes, or just until grill marks appear. Top with blue cheese, if using.

Kale and Potato Hash

A great use of leftover baked potatoes and other vegetables, hash is fast and easy to prepare for breakfast. Using a nonstick skillet allows the potatoes to get crispy as they cook. Serve this hash with eggs.

Serves 4

2 tablespoons canola oil
1 cup diced onion
2 leftover baked Idaho potatoes, cut into 1-inch pieces
3 cloves garlic, minced
½ cup chopped yellow or red bell pepper
4 cups packed de-stemmed, chopped kale
Salt and pepper

If you don't have any leftover baked potatoes, parboil (partially cook) two potatoes in boiling water for 10 to 15 minutes. Remove and allow to cool for 5 minutes. Cut the potatoes into 1-inch pieces.

In a nonstick skillet over medium heat, warm the oil until it shimmers. Cook the onion until translucent, 2 to 3 minutes. Add the potatoes and allow to get crisp on one side. Once crisp, add the garlic and bell pepper, and cook for 2 minutes, stirring occasionally. Add the kale, and cook until it has wilted, about 4 minutes, then season with salt and pepper.

Kale Chips

A popular snack found in grocery stores, these are easy to make at home. This is a basic recipe, but you can experiment with seasonings, such as cayenne, cumin, and garlic powder.

Makes about 4 cups

1 bunch kale, about 4 cups
¼ cup olive oil
1½ teaspoons sea salt
½ teaspoon garlic powder

Preheat the oven to 275°F. Wash the kale and remove the stems. Tear the kale leaves into chip-size pieces. Dry the kale until completely dry, either in a salad spinner or with paper towels or a combination of the two.

In a large bowl, toss the kale with the oil, salt, and garlic powder, making sure to coat every leaf evenly. Working in batches, spread the kale on a baking sheet so that the leaves do not overlap. Bake in the oven until crisp, 15 to 20 minutes. Allow to cool before storing in an airtight container.

Lemony Sautéed Kale

Simple and bright, this recipe is a great way to showcase kale. Try using Meyer lemons when they're in season, as they're a little sweeter. Swiss chard or baby collards also work with this recipe.

Serves 4

1 tablespoon olive oil
½ cup thinly sliced onion
1 clove garlic, minced
4 cups packed de-stemmed, chopped kale
2 tablespoons fresh lemon juice
Salt and pepper

In a large skillet over medium heat, warm the oil until it shimmers. Cook the onion until translucent, about 2 minutes. Add the garlic and cook for 30 seconds. Add the kale and lemon juice, and cook until the kale has wilted, about 4 minutes. Season with salt and pepper to taste. This dish can be stored, covered, in the refrigerator for up to 5 days.

Pickled Kale Stems

This recipe uses all of those castaway stems, creating pickles that are great for salad or sandwich toppings or just for snacking. The quick-pickled stems are ready within 24 hours and are good for one week, covered and refrigerated.

Makes 1 quart

3 cups water
½ cup apple cider vinegar
2 teaspoons salt
1 tablespoon sugar
¼ teaspoon peppercorns
¼ teaspoon red pepper flakes
1 bay leaf
2 allspice berries
10 to 20 stems of kale, cut to fit Mason jar
6 cloves garlic, peeled

Place the water, vinegar, salt, sugar, peppercorns, red pepper flakes, bay leaf, and allspice berries in a 2-quart pot over medium heat. Bring to a boil, stirring until the sugar and salt are dissolved.

Meanwhile, clean the kale stems and cut to fit in a quart-size Mason jar. Place the stems and garlic cloves in the clean jar. Once the pickling liquid is ready, carefully pour it into the jar. Fasten the lid and ring.

Sautéed Radicchio and Endive with Quinoa and Capers

Lemon and capers really complement the flavor of the cooked radicchio and endive. You can use all radicchio or all endive if it is difficult to find either at the grocery store.

Serves 4

1 cup quinoa

2 cups water

Pinch of salt

1 tablespoon olive oil

3 cloves garlic

1 head Belgian or curly endive, diced

1 cup cored and diced radicchio

1 tablespoon capers

1 tablespoon fresh lemon juice

Salt and pepper

2 tablespoons pine nuts

In a small pot over medium heat, combine the quinoa, water, and salt. Bring to a simmer, cover, and cook until the quinoa is tender, 15 to 20 minutes.

In a large skillet over medium heat, warm the oil until it shimmers. Add the garlic, endive, and radicchio. Cook until the greens have wilted, 3 to 4 minutes. Stir in the cooked quinoa, capers, and lemon juice. Season with salt and pepper to taste. In a small pan, over medium-low heat, toast the pine nuts until fragrant and golden brown. Divide the greens and quinoa among four serving plates and top with pine nuts. This can be stored for up to 5 days in the refrigerator.

Chickpeas, Tomatoes, and Rapini

This dish makes a wonderful side, or it can be tossed with pasta or quinoa to make a hearty vegetarian main dish.

Serves 4

1 tablespoon olive oil
1 cup finely diced onion
4 cloves garlic, minced
1 pint cherry tomatoes
5 cups coarsely chopped rapini (about 1 bunch)
1 (15-ounce) can chickpeas, drained and rinsed
2 tablespoons fresh lemon juice
Salt and pepper, to taste
½ teaspoon sugar (optional)

In a large skillet over medium heat, warm the oil until it shimmers. Add the onion and cook for about 8 minutes, or until it begins to turn golden brown. Add the garlic and tomatoes, and cook until the tomatoes blister, about 2 to 3 minutes. Add the rapini, chickpeas, and lemon juice. Continue to cook until the rapini has wilted, about 4 minutes. Season with salt and pepper to taste. If you find the rapini a bit too strongly flavored, you may add the sugar to cut the bitterness.

Broiled Romaine with Parmesan

Primarily served fresh, romaine is also delicious when lightly broiled. The top gets wilted a becomes tender, while the outer leaves retain their crispness. This recipe takes less than 10 minutes to make, from start to finish. Try adding different toppings after broiling, such as bacon, salad dressing, or toasted nuts.

Serves 2

1 head romaine
½ cup grated Parmesan cheese
Pinch of freshly ground black pepper

Preheat the broiler to low. Cut the romaine in half lengthwise. Wash thoroughly and pat dry. Place the romaine on a baking sheet, cut side up. Sprinkle with the Parmesan cheese and season with pepper. Place under the broiler for 2 to 4 minutes, until the cheese has melted and the edges of the romaine leaves begin to turn brown. Serve while still warm.

Vegetable Summer Rolls with Dipping Sauce

No cooking is involved in making these rolls, which makes them perfect for summer or whenever you're in a hurry.

Serves 4

Summer Rolls:

8 leaves romaine or Boston lettuce

16 large basil leaves

16 large mint leaves

4 ounces bean thread rice noodles

1 medium carrot, sliced into matchsticks

1 medium cucumber, sliced into matchsticks

½ medium red bell pepper, sliced into matchsticks

½ cup packed cilantro leaves

16 rice paper wrappers

Dipping Sauce:

1 tablespoon hoisin

1 tablespoon creamy peanut butter

3 tablespoons water

1 teaspoon chili sauce, such as Sriracha

1 teaspoon sugar

1 teaspoon rice vinegar

Cut out any tough stems from the lettuce leaves. Chiffonade the lettuce, and then the basil and the mint, by layering the leaves, rolling them into a tight tube and then slicing in ribbons. Cut the noodles into 2-inch lengths. Soak the noodles in warm water for 6 minutes, then drain.

Fill a wide, shallow dish with enough water to submerge the rice wrappers. Soak one wrapper for 10 to 15 seconds to soften. Spread the wrapper out, then place some lettuce, noodles, and a few carrot, cucumber, and bell pepper matchsticks on the wrapper. Sprinkle some basil, mint, and cilantro on top. Fold the bottom part of the wrapper over the filling, followed by the sides, and then roll from bottom to top to seal. Repeat with the remaining wrappers. Assembled summer rolls are good for 1 day, if kept covered by a moistened paper towel.

Just before serving, make the dipping sauce by whisking together the hoisin, peanut butter, water, chili sauce, sugar, and rice vinegar.

Spinach and Feta Twists

These twists are great for parties as appetizers or as a snack. You can make them easier to eat by cutting the puff pastry in half after rolling it out.

Makes 16 twists

1 tablespoon olive oil

2 tablespoons minced onion

3 cups packed chopped spinach

10 large basil leaves, chopped

1 package frozen puff pastry, thawed

2 tablespoons melted salted butter

Salt and pepper

1 cup crumbled feta cheese

Preheat the oven to 350°F. In a large skillet over medium heat, warm the oil until it shimmers. Add the onion and reduce the heat to low. Cook, stirring occasionally, until the onion is caramelized, 10 to 15 minutes. Add the spinach and basil, cooking only until wilted, about 2 minutes. Season with salt and pepper. Remove from the heat and allow to cool slightly.

Using a rolling pin, roll out the puff pastry sheets on a lightly floured surface until each one is rectangular and about ¼ inch thick. Brush the pastry with melted butter. Spread half of the feta cheese and spinach mixture on to each pastry sheet. Slice the pastry widthwise into 1½-inch strips. Starting at one corner, twist the strip loosely until you reach the other end. Brush the tops with melted butter and place on a baking sheet lined with parchment paper. Bake for 20 to 30 minutes, or until golden brown.

Savory Scones

These scones, which smell fantastic while baking, make a wonderful breakfast. You can substitute other greens, such as kale, chard, or even watercress, in place of spinach.

Serves 8

1 tablespoon olive or canola oil

2 tablespoons minced shallot

3 cups packed spinach

Salt and pepper

2 cups all-purpose flour

1 tablespoon baking powder

1 tablespoon sugar

1 teaspoon salt

5 tablespoons cold unsalted butter

1 cup heavy cream

1 tablespoon Dijon mustard

½ cup Parmesan, pecorino, or other hard cheese

Preheat the oven to 350°F. In a large skillet over medium heat, warm the oil until it shimmers. Add the shallot and cook for 2 minutes, or until it begins to brown on the edges. Add the spinach and cook until wilted, 2 to 3 minutes. Season with salt and pepper to taste.

In a large bowl, mix together the flour, baking powder, sugar, and salt. Using your fingers, work the butter into the flour mixture until there are no distinguishable butter pieces remaining. Add the cooked spinach and stir to coat with the flour. Add the cream, mustard, and cheese, stirring until well combined.

Using your hands, create a ball with the mixture. Place on a baking sheet lined with parchment paper. Pat the ball down, until it is 1 to 1½ inches thick. Cut the flattened ball into eight pie-shaped wedges. Bake for 35 to 45 minutes, until golden brown or until a toothpick inserted into a scone comes out clean. Cooled scones can be stored in an airtight container for 4 days.

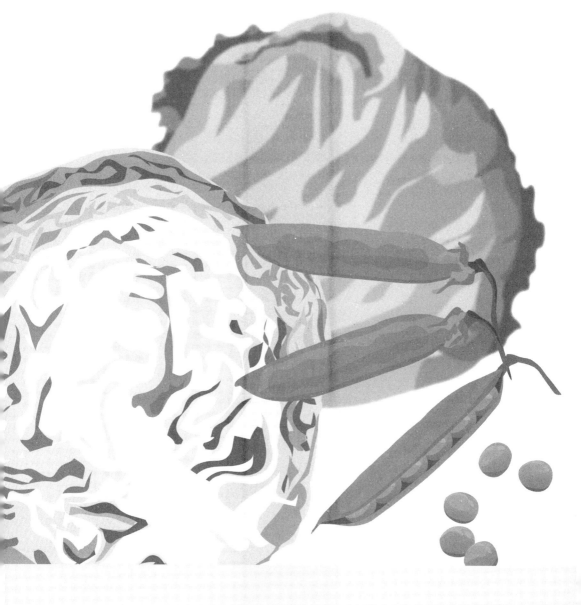

Vegetarian
Entrees

Arugula and Tomato Pizza

Pizza is a fun and easy dinner to prepare. If you want high-quality premade dough, find out if your local pizza place sells some of its dough.

Serves 6

1 (8-ounce) can tomato sauce

½ teaspoon dried oregano

½ teaspoon dried thyme

½ teaspoon sugar

1 ball pizza dough

¾ cup flour

1 tablespoon cornmeal

1 cup shredded mozzarella cheese

1 cup arugula

1 medium Roma tomato, sliced

Preheat the oven to 475°F. In a small pot over medium heat, add the tomato sauce, oregano, thyme, and sugar, and bring to a simmer. Remove from the heat and allow to cool slightly.

Place the pizza dough into a lightly oiled bowl and allow to rise until doubled, about 45 minutes. Dust a clean counter with the flour. Turn the dough out onto the dusted surface and flatten with your hands. Dust a rolling pin and roll the dough into a 12- to 14-inch circle. Sprinkle the cornmeal on a pizza pan or baking sheet before placing the shaped dough on top. Allow the dough to rest for 10 minutes. Spread ½ cup of the tomato sauce mixture on the dough, leaving 1 inch at the edge for the crust. Pinch the edge of the dough to form the crust. Evenly sprinkle on the cheese, and top with the arugula and tomato slices.

Bake for 10 to 15 minutes, or until the crust is golden and the cheese has melted. Allow to cool for 5 minutes before slicing and serving.

Frittata of Baby Greens

Frittatas are similar to omelets, except the filling is cooked into the eggs. This frittata is cooked partway on the stove and finished in the oven.

Serves 4

3 large eggs

¼ cup whole or 2% milk

1 tablespoon unsalted butter

2 tablespoons minced onion

1 clove garlic, minced

2 cups baby lettuce, such as baby kale, spinach, or spring mix

¼ teaspoon salt

⅛ teaspoon black pepper

1 tablespoon chopped chives

¼ cup cheese, such as shredded cheddar or crumbled feta (optional)

Preheat the oven to 350°F. In a medium bowl, whisk together the eggs and milk, and set aside.

In a 6- or 8-inch ovenproof skillet over medium heat, melt the butter. Add the onion and cook until it becomes translucent, 2 to 4 minutes. Toss in the garlic and cook until fragrant, about 30 seconds. Add the lettuce and cook until it just starts to wilt, about 2 minutes. Pour the whisked egg mixture over the wilted lettuce, and reduce the heat to medium-low. With a spatula, push the eggs down the sides of the pan. Season with salt and pepper. Sprinkle with chives and with cheese, if using.

Transfer the skillet to the oven to finish cooking, 5 to 8 minutes, or until the center is set.

Chard Quiche

Quiche is a custard baked in to a shortbread or pastry crust and made with various fillings.

Serves 8

¼ cup shaved Parmesan cheese

1 frozen 9-inch pie shell

1 tablespoon vegetable oil

¼ cup finely diced onion

2 cups packed de-stemmed, chopped Swiss chard

Salt and pepper

6 large eggs

1 teaspoon dried thyme or 2 teaspoons fresh thyme

¾ cup whole or 2% milk

¼ teaspoon salt

¼ teaspoon pepper

¼ cup crumbled goat cheese

Preheat the oven to 350°F. Spread the Parmesan cheese evenly over the bottom of the pie shell.

In a large sauté pan over medium heat, warm the oil until it shimmers. Add the onion and cook until the edges start to brown, about 5 minutes. Add the Swiss chard and cook until wilted, about 3 minutes. Season with salt and pepper to taste. Spread the cooked chard evenly over the Parmesan layer in the pie crust.

In a medium bowl, whisk together the eggs, thyme, milk, salt, and pepper. Gently pour the egg mixture into the pie shell. Sprinkle the crumbled goat cheese on top. Bake for 35 minutes, then, using an instant-read kitchen thermometer, check to see if the internal temperature of the quiche has reached 165°F. If not, continue baking until the center has set and the internal temperature of 165°F is reached.

Garlicky Baby Collards with White Beans and Pasta

The springtime is when baby collards are most abundant. They're great to cook with, as they require much less cooking time than when they are fully grown. You may use spinach, kale, or chard in place of the baby collards.

Serves 4

1 tablespoon salt

2 cups dried pasta, such as fusilli or bow ties

3 tablespoons olive oil

4 cloves garlic, minced

3 cups chopped baby collards

1 cup halved grape or cherry tomatoes

1 (15-ounce) can white beans, such as cannellini or navy, drained and rinsed

Salt and pepper

½ cup shaved or grated Parmesan cheese

Put a large pot of water on the stove to boil, and add the salt. Add the pasta to the boiling water and cook, stirring occasionally, until al dente, about 7 minutes. Drain, saving ½ cup of the cooking water. Shock the pasta in ice water to stop the cooking. Once cooled, drain and set aside.

In a large skillet over medium heat, warm the oil until it shimmers. Add the garlic and collards, and cook until the collards have wilted, about 3 minutes. Add the tomatoes, beans, and cooked pasta, and some pasta cooking water if moisture is needed. Toss together, over medium-low heat, until the tomatoes, beans, and pasta are hot. Season with salt and pepper to taste, divide among plates, and top with the Parmesan cheese.

Gnudi

These dumplings have a light, pillowy texture and are melt-in-your-mouth good. They are especially delicious with brown butter or marinara sauce. You may use spinach, chard, parsley, or other mild-flavored green in place of kale.

Makes 30 to 40 dumplings

1 cup packed de-stemmed, chopped kale or fresh spinach

1 cup ricotta cheese

1 large egg

1 cup shaved Parmesan cheese

¼ cup all-purpose flour, plus ¾ cup for dusting

¼ teaspoon black pepper

Dash of grated nutmeg

Puree the kale or spinach in a blender or food processor. Using a paper towel or cheesecloth, squeeze the moisture from the leaves. Mix together the kale, ricotta, egg, Parmesan, and ¼ cup flour in a medium bowl. Spoon the mixture into a piping bag or large zip-top storage bag and snip off one corner. Spread the remaining ¾ cup flour in a shallow dish. Squeeze out the ricotta mixture 1 tablespoon at a time onto the flour. Dust the tops with flour and smooth the dumpling with your hands.

Bring a small stockpot of water to a rolling boil. Gently drop the dumplings in the water one by one, being careful not to crowd the pot. With a slotted spoon, remove the dumplings from the water once they begin to float, about 1½ minutes.

The ricotta mixture can be made 1 day ahead and stored in the refrigerator. Cooked gnudi should be eaten the same day.

Roasted Radicchio and Mushrooms with Pasta

Roasting radicchio brings out its sweetness and makes it almost creamy. Mushrooms enhance the earthy flavor. The best mushrooms are ones like hen-of-the-woods (maitake) or morels, but white mushrooms or cremini will work, too.

Serves 4

2 heads radicchio, cut into a total of 12 wedges

2 cups sliced mushrooms

4 tablespoons olive oil, divided

2 cloves garlic, minced

½ pound dried short pasta, such as fusilli or cavatappi

1 cup diced onion (about 1 small onion)

½ teaspoon anchovy paste (optional)

¼ cup chopped parsley

½ teaspoon red pepper flakes

Salt and pepper

½ cup shaved Parmesan cheese (optional)

Preheat the oven to 475°F. Place the radicchio wedges and mushrooms on a baking pan, and gently toss with 2 tablespoons oil and the garlic. Roast for 20 to 25 minutes, or until the radicchio and mushrooms begin to brown.

Bring a large pot of water to a boil. Add the salt and the pasta. Stirring every couple of minutes, cook the pasta until al dente, about 7 minutes. Shock the pasta in an ice bath until it is cool, then drain and set aside.

Heat the remaining 2 tablespoons oil in a large sauté pan. Cook the onion for 3 minutes, or until translucent, stirring occasionally. Stir in the anchovy paste, if using, then add the roasted radicchio and mushrooms, cooked pasta, parsley, and red pepper flakes. Season with salt and pepper to taste. Divide among serving dishes, then top with Parmesan cheese, if desired.

This dish can be stored, covered, in the refrigerator for up to 5 days.

Rapini with Caramelized Onions and Creamy Polenta

This combination is popular in Italy. Rapini is abundant in the spring, but if you have trouble finding it, you may substitute mustard greens, dandelion greens, or other bitter greens.

Serves 6

2 tablespoons olive oil, divided

1 large onion, halved and thinly sliced

6 cups water

1½ cups cornmeal

2 tablespoons unsalted butter

6 cups trimmed, chopped rapini, in 1-inch pieces

1 tablespoon apple cider vinegar

Salt and pepper

In a large skillet over medium heat, warm 1 tablespoon of the oil until it shimmers. Add the onion and cook for 30 to 45 minutes, stirring occasionally, until dark brown. If the pan gets too dry while cooking, add 1 tablespoon water.

Meanwhile, make the polenta by bringing 6 cups water to a boil in a large pot. Add the cornmeal in a slow and steady stream to the boiling water while whisking with the other hand. Continue to whisk for an additional minute to get rid of any lumps. Reduce the heat to low and cook the cornmeal, stirring every 2 minutes, until tender and thick, about 15 minutes. Turn off the heat, stir in the butter, and season with salt and pepper to taste.

When the onions are through cooking, transfer them to a bowl. In a medium skillet, heat the remaining 1 tablespoon oil over medium heat until it shimmers. Add the rapini and cook until wilted, about 5 minutes. If the pan gets too dry, add 1 tablespoon water. Once the rapini has wilted, add the vinegar and return the onion to the skillet. Season with salt and pepper to taste. Stir together and serve over the polenta.

Spinach and Ricotta Stuffed Shells

A simple dinner that can easily be doubled or tripled and stored in the freezer. You may use kale or chard in place of the spinach.

Serves 4 or 5

Sauce:

1 teaspoon olive oil

1 large shallot, minced

4 cloves garlic, minced

1 (28-ounce) can crushed tomatoes

1 tablespoon tomato paste

1 teaspoon dried thyme

1 teaspoon dried oregano

1 teaspoon dried basil

½ teaspoon red pepper flakes

Salt and pepper

Stuffed Pasta Shells:

1 tablespoon salt

20 large pasta shells, about ½ package

1 teaspoon olive oil

½ cup finely diced onion

10 ounces frozen spinach, thawed and drained

1 teaspoon dried oregano or 2 teaspoons fresh oregano

1 (15-ounce) container ricotta cheese

¾ cup shaved Parmesan cheese, divided

2 eggs

Pinch of salt

Pinch of pepper

¼ cup mozzarella cheese

Preheat the oven to 350°F. To make the sauce, in a 3-quart pot over medium heat, warm the oil until it shimmers. Add the shallot and garlic, and cook 15 to 20 seconds, until fragrant. Add the crushed tomatoes, tomato paste, thyme, oregano, basil, and red pepper flakes. Stir, reduce the heat to low, and simmer for 10 minutes. Season with salt and pepper to taste.

Bring a stock pot of salted water to a boil and add the shells. Cook, stirring occasionally, for about 10 minutes, or until the pasta shells are al dente. Drain and run under cold water until the pasta is cool. Set aside.

To prepare the filling, in a large sauté pan over medium heat, warm the oil until it shimmers. Cook the onion for about 2 minutes, until it becomes translucent. Add the spinach and oregano, and cook for an additional 2 to 3 minutes. Drain any excess liquid and transfer to a food processor. Process the spinach mixture until it has an even consistency. In a large bowl, mix together the ricotta, ½ cup of the Parmesan cheese, and the eggs. Add the spinach mixture, and mix until well combined. Season with the salt and pepper.

Fill each pasta shell with about 2 tablespoons of the spinach and cheese mixture. Place the stuffed shells into 9 x 13-inch baking dish. Pour the sauce over the shells. Bake, covered, for 20 minutes. Uncover and sprinkle the mozzarella and the remaining ¼ cup Parmesan over top. Bake uncovered for an additional 10 minutes, or until the cheeses have melted. This may be stored, covered, in the refrigerator for up to 5 days, or can be frozen in individual portions for up to 3 months.

Spinach Burgers

Low in fat, high in protein and vitamins, these burgers are gluten free and guilt free. You can serve them on buns or over pasta or grains.

Serves 4

3 tablespoons olive oil, divided

½ cup finely diced onion

2 cloves garlic, minced

3 cups packed chopped spinach

1 (15-ounce) can cannellini beans, drained and rinsed

½ cup cooked white or brown rice

Salt and pepper

In a large sauté pan or skillet over medium heat, warm 1 tablespoon of the oil until it shimmers. Add the onion and cook until translucent, about 2 minutes. Toss in the garlic and cook for 30 seconds. Add the spinach and cook until wilted, about 3 minutes. In a food processor, mix together the spinach mixture and beans, pulsing until well combined. Scrape out into a large bowl, mix with the rice, and season with salt and pepper to taste. Divide the mixture into 4 patties. Heat the remaining 2 tablespoons oil in a medium sauté pan or skillet and cook the patties until they begin to brown, then flip to brown the other side, about 4 minutes per side.

Hot Spinach, Mozzarella, and Tomato on Ciabatta

This sandwich features crisp bread, gooey cheese, and fresh spinach and tomato. Its fast assembly is another bonus! You can use kale or baby lettuces in place of the spinach, if desired.

Serves 1

2 teaspoons Dijon mustard

6-inch ciabatta loaf sliced lengthwise

¼ cup shredded mozzarella cheese

1 medium Roma tomato, thinly sliced

½ cup packed fresh spinach

Pinch of black pepper

Spread a thin layer of mustard on both slices of the bread then evenly sprinkle the cheese. On a small baking sheet, toast the bread and melt the cheese, either in the oven or a toaster oven set to broil. Remove from the oven, and layer 1 slice of the bread with tomato and the other with spinach. Season with a small pinch of pepper, then close the two slices of bread together.

Spinach and Potato Pierogies

These are Polish dumplings, often served at holidays and on special occasions. They are best made with a friend or family member helping to roll, fill, and seal.

Makes 40 to 50 dumplings

Filling:

2 Idaho potatoes, peeled and diced

¼ cup whole or 2% milk

1 tablespoon olive oil

½ cup diced onion

2 cups packed chopped spinach

Salt and pepper

2 tablespoons melted butter (optional, for frying)

Dough:

2 large eggs

1 cup sour cream

2½ cups all-purpose flour

½ teaspoon salt

Bring a medium pot of water to a boil. Cook the potatoes for 10 minutes, or until fork tender. Drain, return to the pot, add the milk, and mash. You want the potatoes to have a smooth consistency, but if they are overprocessed, the potatoes will become very tacky and gummy.

In a large skillet over medium heat, warm the oil until it shimmers. Cook the onion until the edges begin to brown, about 5 minutes. Add the spinach and cook until wilted, 2 to 3 minutes. Season with salt and pepper to taste. In a blender or food processor, puree the cooked spinach mixture. Add the blended spinach and melted butter to the mashed potatoes, stirring to combine.

To make the dough, mix together the eggs and sour cream, then sift in the flour and salt. Mix until well combined. Cut the dough in half, and form two balls. Cover with plastic wrap and allow to rest for 30 minutes. With a lightly floured rolling pin, roll out one ball of dough until very thin, preferably 1⁄16 inch thick. Cut out rounds using a 3-inch biscuit cutter. Place 2 tablespoons of filling in the center of each dough round. Dampen the edge of the dough, fold over, and seal by crimping the edges with a fork.

To fry: In a large skillet over medium heat, warm 2 tablespoons butter and fry the pierogies until golden brown on each side.

To boil: Bring a large pot of salted water to a boil. Gently drop in the pierogies, making sure not to crowd the pot, and boil until they begin to float.

Serve with a dollop of sour cream, fried onions, or melted butter.

Saag Paneer

This is an Indian dish made with spinach, fresh cheese curds, and spices. The characteristic flavor comes from the spice blend garam masala, which is usually a combination of peppercorns, cloves, cinnamon, cumin, and cardamom. You can find this spice blend in most grocery stores, but can make your own if you're feeling ambitious and have a mortar and pestle.

Serves 4

8 cups whole milk

3 tablespoons fresh lemon juice

2 tablespoons olive oil

1 cup diced onion

3 cloves garlic, minced

1 tablespoon minced fresh ginger

1 serrano chile pepper, seeded and sliced (optional)

4 cups packed fresh spinach

1 tablespoon garam masala

½ teaspoon cayenne pepper

½ teaspoon ground turmeric

Salt and pepper

In a large pot over medium heat, warm the milk to a simmer. Stir in the lemon juice 1 tablespoon at a time. Once curds have formed, remove the pot from the heat. Line a colander or strainer with two layers of cheesecloth, and slowly pour in the curdled milk. Allow to drain for 30 minutes. Gently squeeze the cloth to remove excess moisture, then fold the cheesecloth over the top of the curds and place a weighted object, such as a heavy pot, on top. Allow to drain for an additional 30 to 60 minutes. Unwrap the paneer cheese and cut into cubes. Use immediately or cover with water and store in the refrigerator for up to 1 week.

In a large sauté pan over medium heat, warm the oil until it shimmers. Add the onion and cook until the edges begin to brown, about 5 minutes. Add the garlic, ginger, and chile pepper, if using, and cook for 30 seconds. Add the spinach, garam masala, cayenne, and turmeric. Cook until the spinach has wilted, 2 to 3 minutes. Using a food processor or blender, puree the spinach mixture, return it to the pan, then gently stir in the paneer cheese. Add up to ¼ cup water if a smoother consistency is desired. Season with salt and pepper to taste. Serve over rice or another grain.

Swiss Chard and Egg Breakfast Burrito

A quick and filling breakfast, this dish takes less than 10 minutes to make. You can substitute kale or collard greens for the Swiss chard.

Serves 1

1 tablespoon olive oil

1 teaspoon minced shallot

1 clove garlic, minced

2 large Swiss chard leaves, de-stemmed and chopped

1 (10-inch) flour tortilla

2 tablespoons shredded cheddar or pepper Jack cheese

2 large eggs

Salt and pepper

1 tablespoon prepared salsa

1 pickled kale stem, diced (optional; see page 51)

In a small, nonstick sauté pan or skillet over medium heat, warm the oil until it shimmers. Add the shallot and cook until translucent, about 2 minutes. Toss in the garlic and cook for 30 seconds. Add the Swiss chard and cook until it begins to wilt, about 3 minutes. Remove from the heat.

Place the tortilla in a dry skillet large enough to hold it and sprinkle on the cheese. Place the cooked chard mixture in a line down the center of the tortilla, and turn the heat on low.

Crack the eggs into a small bowl and beat with a fork. Pour the eggs into a small nonstick pan and turn the heat to medium. With a rubber spatula, continuously stir the eggs until they form curds and are cooked to the desired doneness. Season with salt and pepper to taste. Scoop the eggs over the chard, and top with salsa and pickled kale stem, if using. Fold the tortilla over the filling, first the top, then the sides and then the bottom.

Swiss Chard with Raisins and Pine Nuts

This recipe features the classic way of preparing greens in Italy. You can substitute kale, collard greens, or spinach for the Swiss chard.

Serves 4

¼ cup raisins
¼ cup hot water
1 tablespoon olive oil
½ cup diced onion
6 cups packed de-stemmed, chopped Swiss chard
Salt and pepper
¼ cup pine nuts

In a small bowl, soak the raisins in the hot water until plump, about 10 minutes. Reserve the water in which the raisins soaked.

In a small dry sauté pan over medium-low heat, toast the pine nuts until fragrant and golden brown. Remove from the heat and set aside to cool.

In a large skillet over medium heat, warm the oil until it shimmers. Add the onion and cook until it begins to brown, 4 to 5 minutes. Add the chard and plumped raisins, and cook until the chard has wilted, about 3 minutes. If desired, add 1 or 2 tablespoons of the raisin water to help wilt the chard. Season with salt and pepper to taste. Toss the cooked chard with the pine nuts.

This dish can be stored in the refrigerator, covered, for up to 5 days.

Root Vegetable Risotto with Turnip Greens

Risotto is an Italian rice dish typically made with Arborio rice. Many different ingredients may be mixed in, such as meat, seafood, or, in this case, root vegetables and turnip greens.

Serves 4

Roasted Root Vegetables:

1 small parsnip

3 medium red radishes

1 medium turnip

2 tablespoons olive oil

Salt and pepper

Risotto:

2 tablespoons olive oil

1 small onion, finely diced

1 clove garlic, minced

1 cup Arborio rice

4 cups chicken or vegetable broth, or water, divided

1 cup packed chopped turnip greens

½ cup grated Parmesan cheese

Salt and pepper

Preheat the oven to 400°F. Peel and dice the parsnip, radishes, and turnip into ½-inch pieces and place on a baking pan. Toss with the olive oil, and season with a pinch each of salt and pepper. Roast the vegetables for 20 to 30 minutes, or until tender.

To make the risotto, in a 3-quart or larger pot over medium heat, warm the olive oil until it shimmers. Add the onion and cook until it starts to soften, about 1 minute. Add the garlic and the Arborio rice. Stir to coat the rice in oil, and cook for 1 minute, until the garlic becomes fragrant. Add 2 cups of the broth or water. Bring to a boil, then reduce heat to low. Simmer, uncovered, for an additional 15 to 20 minutes, stirring every 2 to 3 minutes, until the rice is cooked through. Add more liquid, ½ cup at a time, as needed.

Stir the roasted root vegetables, Parmesan cheese, and turnip greens into the cooked risotto. Season with salt and pepper to taste.

Poultry, Fish, **and** Meat**Entrees**

Stir-Fried Bok Choy with Beef

A good weeknight standby, this is superfast to throw together for your family. You can use chicken or tofu instead of beef.

Serves 4

1 tablespoon sesame oil
1 cup finely diced onion
3 cloves garlic, minced
1 tablespoon minced fresh ginger
½ pound sirloin steak, cut into 1-inch strips
Black pepper
2 tablespoons soy sauce
1 tablespoon cornstarch
2 tablespoons water
6 cups packed chopped bok choy

In a large skillet or wok over medium-high heat, warm the oil until it shimmers. Sauté the onion until it begins to brown, 3 to 4 minutes, then reduce the heat to medium-low and add the garlic and ginger, cooking for an additional 30 seconds. Season the steak strips with black pepper, then add them to the skillet, cooking for about 1 minute, stirring occasionally, or until almost cooked through. In a small bowl, mix together the soy sauce, cornstarch, and water. Add the bok choy to the skillet, cooking for 3 minutes, then add the soy and cornstarch mixture. Bring to a simmer, allowing the sauce to thicken slightly. Season with black pepper to taste, and stir to coat. Serve over rice or other grains. This is best eaten immediately after preparing, but can be stored in the refrigerator for up to 5 days.

Corned Beef and Cabbage

This is a classic Irish dish that can simmer on the stove and requires very little additional attention. The meat is tender and falls apart with just a fork.

Serves 4 to 6

3½ pounds corned beef brisket

12 cups (3 quarts) beef broth or water, divided

2 bay leaves

1 teaspoon peppercorns

4 allspice berries

1 small onion, quartered

1 large carrot, quartered

2 ribs celery, cut into 2-inch pieces

4 small whole Yukon Gold potatoes

1 small head green cabbage

1 (15-ounce) can beer, such as Guinness

In a large stockpot, combine the corned beef, 4 cups (1 quart) of the stock or water, and the bay leaves, peppercorns, and allspice berries, and cover with a lid. Simmer on low heat for 2 hours, adding more liquid if needed. Add the remaining ingredients, cover, and continue to simmer for an additional 2 hours. Allow to cool for 15 to 20 minutes before serving.

Chicken and Cabbage Wontons

Wontons are surprisingly easy and fun to make, especially when you have help sealing all of the wrappers. This can be made vegetarian by omitting the chicken and increasing the amount of cabbage to 4 cups.

Serves 8

1 tablespoon sesame oil

1 small onion, minced

3 cloves garlic, minced

1 tablespoon minced fresh ginger

¼ pound ground chicken

2 cups shredded green cabbage

½ cup diced scallion, trimmed

1 teaspoon oyster sauce

2 tablespoons soy sauce

Black pepper

4 cups canola or peanut oil

2 tablespoons water

2 tablespoons cornstarch

1 package wonton wrappers

In a large skillet over medium heat, warm the sesame oil until it shimmers. Sauté the onion until translucent, about 3 minutes. Add the garlic and ginger, cooking for 30 seconds. Add the ground chicken, breaking up any large chunks with a spatula, and cook for 5 to 7 minutes, or until cooked through. Add the cabbage, scallion, oyster sauce, and soy sauce, and cook until the cabbage has wilted, about 3 minutes. Season with pepper to taste and turn off the heat.

Meanwhile, in a small stockpot over medium heat, warm the canola or peanut oil until it reaches 350°F, but not more than 375°F. Check the temperature with a high-heat kitchen thermometer. In a small bowl, mix together the water and cornstarch. Working with 4 wonton wrappers at a time, lay out the wrappers with one point facing you. Place 1 tablespoon of the chicken and cabbage filling in the top center of the wrapper. Dip your finger into the cornstarch and water mixture and dampen the top two edges. Fold the bottom over the filling and seal the edges together. Gently slide the sealed wontons into the hot oil and fry until they begin to turn golden brown. Remove and drain on paper towels. Repeat filling, sealing, and frying the wontons in batches of 4 until all the filling is used. Replace the paper towels as they become saturated with oil.

The wontons are best enjoyed fresh, but they can be reheated for 5 to 8 minutes in an oven at 400°F.

Pork-Stuffed Cabbage Rolls

This is sometimes called pigs in a blanket and is common in Eastern European countries and the Middle East.

Makes 10 rolls

10 whole cabbage leaves
1 tablespoon olive oil
1 small onion, finely diced
3 cloves garlic, minced
½ pound ground pork
1 tablespoon tomato paste
1 large egg, beaten
Salt and pepper
1 (8-ounce) can tomato sauce
1 (14-ounce) can diced
   tomatoes
1 tablespoon sugar

Preheat the oven to 350°F. Bring a large pot of water to a boil. Blanch the cabbage leaves by placing them in the boiling water until they are soft, 2 to 3 minutes, then removing them and running them under cold water. Once cooled, pat dry and set aside.

In a large skillet over medium heat, warm the oil until it shimmers. Cook the onion for about 1 minute. Add the garlic and pork, breaking up large chunks with a spatula, and cook for 4 to 6 minutes, or until the pork is cooked through. Transfer the pork mixture to a bowl, removing any excess liquid. Season with salt and pepper. Stir in the tomato paste and beaten egg.

In a medium bowl, mix together the tomato sauce, diced tomatoes, sugar, and salt and pepper to taste.

Lay out the cabbage leaves. Place about ¼ cup of the pork mixture on each leaf, near the thick stem. Roll each cabbage leaf over the pork mixture and tuck in the sides. Place the cabbage rolls in a 9 x 13-inch baking dish. Spread the tomato mixture evenly over the cabbage rolls. Cover with aluminum foil and bake for 40 to 45 minutes, until the internal temperature has reached 145°F when measured with a kitchen thermometer.

Fish and Chard en Papillote

En papillote means "in parchment" in French, but you can use aluminum foil instead. The food is steamed in its own juices, which translates to lots of flavor without added fat.

Serves 4

4 cups packed de-stemmed, chopped Swiss chard

4 (8-ounce) fish fillets, such salmon, halibut, or tuna

Salt and pepper

1 tablespoon dried thyme

4 scallions, both white and green parts, finely sliced

¼ cup packed chopped parsley

2 medium lemons, sliced

Preheat the oven to 350°F. Rip off four square pieces from a roll of aluminum foil or parchment paper. In the center of each piece, place 1 cup Swiss chard and top with 1 fish fillet. Season the fish with a pinch each of salt and pepper. Divide the thyme, scallions, and parsley among the fish fillets. Place 2 slices of lemon on top of each fillet. Fold the foil or parchment over the fish, crimping along the edges to create a seal. Place the packets on a baking sheet and bake for 10 to 15 minutes, or until the fish is cooked. Serve in the packets.

Store any leftovers, covered but removed from the aluminum foil or parchment, for up to 3 days in the refrigerator.

Chicken-Stuffed Endive

Belgian endive leaves are shaped perfectly for fillings. This recipe uses ground chicken, but you could use ground turkey, pork, lamb, or beef too.

Serves 4

3 heads Belgian endive
½ pound ground chicken
½ cup Italian bread crumbs
1 tablespoon minced fresh parsley
1 tablespoon dried thyme
1 teaspoon dried rosemary
2 cloves garlic, minced
1 small egg, beaten
Pinch of salt
Pinch of pepper
½ cup grated Gruyère or Parmesan cheese

Preheat the oven to 350°F. Trim the bottoms off the endive heads, and remove the outer leaves, placing them face up on a baking sheet.

In a medium bowl, mix together the chicken, bread crumbs, parsley, thyme, rosemary, garlic, and beaten egg. Season with salt and pepper.

Fill each endive leaf with about 2 tablespoons of the chicken mixture. Sprinkle the cheese evenly over top and bake, uncovered, for 10 to 15 minutes, or until cooked through.

This dish is best eaten fresh, but can be stored in the refrigerator for up to 5 days.

Kale and Chicken Enchiladas

Enchiladas are often filled with just meat and/or cheese. Kale helps to lighten up this dish and adds more nutrients. To make this dish vegetarian, use black beans in place of the chicken.

Serves 8

2 tablespoons olive oil, divided

1 pound boneless, skinless chicken breasts

Salt and pepper

1 cup finely chopped onion

3 cloves garlic, minced

3 cups packed de-stemmed, chopped kale

½ cup finely diced red bell pepper

2 chipotle chile peppers, seeded and diced

1 (28-ounce) can diced tomatoes

1 teaspoon ground cumin

½ teaspoon dried oregano or 1 teaspoon fresh oregano

½ teaspoon chili powder

1 (10-ounce) can enchilada sauce, divided

8 (8-inch) flour or corn tortillas

½ cup shredded cheddar or pepper Jack cheese

¼ cup packed cilantro (optional)

1 lime, cut into wedges (optional)

Sour cream (optional)

Preheat the oven to 400°F. In a large skillet over medium heat, warm 1 tablespoon of the oil until it shimmers. Season the chicken with a pinch each of salt and pepper. Add it to the skillet and cook for 4 minutes on each side, or until cooked through. Remove from the pan and allow to cool for 8 minutes. Using two forks, shred the chicken.

Wipe out the skillet, return to medium heat, and heat the remaining 1 tablespoon oil. Cook the onion until translucent, about 3 minutes. Add the garlic, kale, bell pepper, chile pepper, tomato, shredded chicken, cumin, oregano, and chili powder. Season with salt and pepper to taste. Once the kale has wilted, about 3 minutes, turn off the heat.

Spread ¼ cup enchilada sauce on the bottom of a 9 x 13-inch baking dish. Spread 1 tablespoon of sauce in the center of a tortilla. Fill the tortilla with ⅓ cup of the kale and chicken filling, then roll it, leaving the ends open. Place the filled tortilla in the sauce-covered baking dish. Repeat with the remaining tortillas and filling. Pour the remaining enchilada sauce over the filled tortillas in the baking dish, sprinkle the cheese over the top, and bake, uncovered, for 8 to 10 minutes, or until the cheese has melted. Allow to cool for 5 minutes before serving.

If desired, top with cilantro, and lime wedges, and a dollop of sour cream.

Mustard Greens with Pork

A minimalist recipe that is very flavorful and easy to make, this is an ideal weeknight dinner. It can be made vegetarian by substituting firm tofu in place of the pork. Serve this over rice or another grain to complete the meal.

Serves 4

6 cups packed de-stemmed, chopped mustard greens
1 teaspoon salt
1 pound ground pork
1 tablespoon sesame oil
1 small onion, finely diced
2 tablespoons soy sauce

Sprinkle the mustard greens with the salt and bruise them gently with your hands. Allow the salt to wilt the greens for 15 minutes. Drain and squeeze any water that may come out of the greens. Cut in to 1-inch ribbons.

In a medium skillet over medium heat, cook the pork, breaking it up with a spoon. Drain the fat from the pork and set it aside. In a medium sauté pan, heat the oil over medium heat until it shimmers. Add the onion and cook until it becomes translucent, 2 to 3 minutes. Add the cooked pork, mustard greens, and soy sauce, stirring to combine and cooking for 2 to 3 minutes.

Flank Steak Roll with Miso Mustard Greens

This Asian-inspired steak packs a lot of flavor, thanks to the mustard greens and miso. Miso is fermented soy bean paste and can be found in the refrigerated section of your grocery store.

Serves 4

Marinated Steak:

1½ pounds flank steak

¼ cup olive oil

½ cup soy sauce

½ cup rice vinegar

1 tablespoon minced garlic

1 tablespoon minced fresh ginger

Miso Mustard Greens:

1 tablespoon olive oil

1 large shallot, minced

2 cloves garlic, minced

6 cups packed de-stemmed, chopped mustard greens

1 cup water

2 tablespoons miso paste

Preheat the oven to 450°F. With a sharp knife, carefully butterfly the flank steak by laying the meat flat on a cutting board and slicing into the side of the meat, almost all the way through. This makes the meat thinner and larger, which makes it easier to roll around the mustard greens. In a bowl or food-grade bag large enough to hold the steak, mix the marinade of olive oil, soy sauce, rice vinegar, garlic, and ginger. Add the steak. Cover and refrigerate for 15 to 30 minutes.

In a medium sauté pan over medium heat, warm 1 tablespoon oil until it simmers. Cook the shallot and garlic until the shallot begins to turn translucent, 1 to 2 minutes. Add the mustard greens. In a small bowl, mix together the water and miso, then add to the mustard greens. Reduce the heat to low and continue to simmer until the mustard greens have wilted, about 2 minutes. Drain the liquid from the wilted greens and turn off the heat.

Remove the steak from the marinade and pat dry with a paper towel. Spread the mustard greens mixture evenly over the steak, leaving ½ inch on all edges. Roll the steak toward you, with the grain going from left to right. Tie or truss the steak so that it cooks evenly. In a hot sauté pan, sear the steak for about 4 minutes on all sides. Place in an ovenproof baking dish and roast for 15 minutes, or until the internal temperature reaches 165°F. Let the meat rest for 10 minutes before slicing across the grain.

Szechuan Mustard Greens with Shrimp

Szechuan cuisine originates from the Sichuan province of China. It is characterized by ample use of chile peppers and garlic. This dish is great served over a grain such as rice, barley, or quinoa.

Serves 4

8 cloves garlic, minced

1 tablespoon grated fresh ginger

½ cup soy sauce

¼ cup chili paste, such as sambal

2 tablespoons red pepper flakes

2 tablespoons sesame oil

6 cups packed de-stemmed, chopped mustard greens

1 pound shrimp, shells removed and deveined

To make the Szechuan sauce, in a small bowl, mix together the garlic, ginger, soy sauce, chili paste, and red pepper flakes. In a large skillet over medium heat, warm the sesame oil until it shimmers. Add the mustard greens and the Szechuan sauce. Cook, stirring, until the greens have wilted, 3 to 4 minutes. Remove the greens from the pan, and add the shrimp. Cook just until the shrimp turn opaque, 3 to 4 minutes. Return the mustard greens to the pan and toss to combine the greens, shrimp, and sauce.

Croque-Monsieur with Rapini

What is better than a hot ham and cheese sandwich? One with the crunch and spicy flavor of rapini. Top this dish with a fried egg to make it a croque-madame.

Serves 2

Béchamel Sauce:

2 tablespoons unsalted butter

2 tablespoons all-purpose flour

1 cup whole milk

2 tablespoons grated Parmesan cheese

2 tablespoons grated Gruyère cheese

Pinch of grated nutmeg

Pinch of salt

Pinch of pepper

Sandwich:

1 teaspoon olive oil

1 clove garlic, minced

2 cups chopped rapini

Salt and pepper

4 slices hearty white bread

2 tablespoons Dijon mustard

¼ cup grated Gruyère cheese

4 slices ham

To make the béchamel sauce, in a small pot over low heat, melt the butter and whisk in the flour. Cook until the mixture bubbles, and then whisk in the milk. Bring to a simmer. Stir in the cheeses, and season with the nutmeg and salt and pepper. Stir until the cheeses have melted. Remove from the heat.

To prepare the sandwich filling, in a large sauté pan over medium heat, warm the oil until it shimmers. Add the garlic and cook until fragrant, about 30 seconds. Add the rapini and cook until it is wilted, 4 to 5 minutes. Season with salt and pepper to taste.

Toast the bread until golden brown. Preheat the oven's broiler to low. Place the bread on to a baking sheet. Spread the mustard on two slices of toasted bread. Place the Gruyère cheese on top of the mustard, and then top with the ham and the cooked rapini mixture. Top with the remaining slices of bread and pour the béchamel sauce evenly over top. Set under the broiler until the tops are bubbly and lightly browned, 1 to 2 minutes. Be careful to keep a close eye on the sandwiches while they are in the broiler, as they can go from perfect to burnt very quickly.

Spinach-Stuffed Chicken Breast Wrapped in Bacon

Stuffing spinach inside of the chicken makes a very pretty presentation when sliced open. The bacon keeps the chicken very moist during cooking and adds a little crunch. You can use kale or chard in place of the spinach.

Serves 4

1 tablespoon olive oil
1 cup finely diced onion
4 cloves garlic, minced
6 cups packed fresh spinach
Pinch of salt
Pinch of pepper
½ teaspoon red pepper flakes (optional)
4 boneless, skinless chicken breasts (1 to 1½ pounds)
4 slices bacon

Preheat the oven to 350°F. In a large sauté pan over medium heat, warm the oil until it shimmers. Add the onion and cook until translucent, 2 or 3 minutes. Toss in the garlic and cook for 30 seconds. Add the spinach and cook until wilted, about 2 minutes. Season with salt and pepper to taste, and with red pepper flakes, if desired.

Lay the chicken breasts flat. Using a paring knife, carefully slice a pocket into side of each breast, starting from the thickest side, without slicing all the way through. Insert equal amounts of cooked spinach mixture into the chicken breasts. Fold the chicken over and season with salt and pepper. Wrap a slice of bacon around each breast and secure with cooking twine.

In a large ovenproof skillet over medium heat, cook the chicken breasts for 3 minutes on each side, or until browned. Transfer the skillet to the oven and bake until the internal temperature reaches 160°F when measured with a kitchen thermometer, 15 to 20 minutes. Allow some carry-over cooking for a couple of minutes before removing the twine. Slice on an angle to showcase the bacon, chicken, and spinach layers. The cooked chicken breasts can be stored, covered, in the refrigerator for up to 5 days.

Watercress and Salmon Coconut Curry

This recipe uses Thai green curry paste, which is made with ingredients like green chilies, kaffir leaves, cilantro, and shrimp paste. You can find premade green curry paste in the Asian section of your grocery store or online at thaikitchen.com

Serves 4

1 tablespoon olive oil

1 cup diced onion

2 cloves garlic, minced

1 teaspoon minced fresh ginger

1 tablespoon green curry paste

1 (15-ounce) can light coconut milk

1 cup chicken or vegetable broth

1 stalk fresh lemongrass or 2 (3-inch) dried stalks

1 pound salmon, cut into bite-size pieces

2 cups packed watercress, large stems removed

10 large basil leaves, chopped

Salt and pepper

In a large skillet over medium heat, warm the oil until it shimmers. Add the onion and cook until it becomes translucent, 3 to 4 minutes. Add the garlic, ginger, and curry paste, cooking for 30 seconds. Stir in the coconut milk and broth. Bruise the lemongrass stalk by hitting it with something heavy, such as a muddling stick or tenderizing hammer, before adding it to the curry sauce. Bring to a simmer and stir in the salmon. Continue cooking for 3 to 4 minutes, then add the watercress and basil. Cook for an additional 3 to 4 minutes, until the watercress is wilted. Taste the sauce before seasoning it with salt and pepper, as the curry paste may add enough saltiness. Serve over rice or another grain.

This can be stored, covered, in the refrigerator for up to 3 days.

Watercress and Herb Sauce over Salmon

This watercress and herb sauce pairs well with seafood but it also goes well with chicken. It is almost effortless, and this recipe takes no more than 15 minutes to prepare.

Serves 4

2 cups packed watercress, large stems removed

10 large basil leaves

1 cup packed parsley

2 cloves garlic

½ cup plus 1 tablespoon olive oil, divided

½ cup water

¼ cup fresh lemon juice

1 pound salmon, cut into 4 pieces

Salt and pepper

2 scallions, diced (optional)

In a blender, combine the watercress, basil, parsley, garlic, ½ cup olive oil, water, and lemon juice. Blend until smooth. Season with salt and pepper to taste.

Pat the salmon dry and season with a pinch each of salt and pepper. In a skillet over medium heat, warm 1 tablespoon olive oil until it shimmers. Gently place the salmon in the pan. Cook for 3 to 4 minutes, depending on thickness, on each side, or until desired doneness. Plate each piece of salmon and top with watercress sauce. If desired, garnish with scallions.

The sauce can be stored in the refrigerator, covered, for up to 1 week, and the cooked salmon for up to 3 days.

Juices and Smoothies

Blueberry Bok Choy Smoothie

Bok choy has a very mild flavor, which makes it a good addition to any smoothie. It also adds extra vitamins and fiber.

Serves 1

1 cup frozen blueberries
½ cup plain or vanilla yogurt
½ cup orange juice
1 cup packed chopped bok choy

Place all the ingredients in a blender, and blend until smooth.

Chard, Beet, and Carrot Juice

In juices, chard has a very vegetal flavor, which is similar to spinach, kale, or parsley. A Granny Smith apple is added for sweetness and tartness, but you may use other varieties, if you prefer.

Serves 1

3 whole, large Swiss chard leaves
1 large beet
2 large carrots
½ medium Granny Smith apple

Cut the ingredients into pieces manageable for your juicer. Juice each ingredient, in the order listed.

Red Chard and Strawberry Smoothie

This bright red smoothie utilizes all those Swiss chard stems that were removed in other recipes. It has a pretty mild flavor and is not too sweet. Add a little honey if you prefer a sweeter treat.

Serves 2

1 cup apple juice or cider

8 Swiss chard stems

8 large strawberries, frozen

1 tablespoon fresh lemon juice

1 (6-ounce) container plain or vanilla yogurt

Place the apple juice or cider, Swiss chard stems, and strawberries in a blender, and blend until smooth. Add the lemon juice and yogurt, blending for an additional 2 or 3 seconds, to combine.

Dandelion Fruit Juice

Dandelion greens are best used in spring, when the leaves are smaller and more mild flavored. They can be bitter at other times of the year. Adding the apple brings some sweetness and balances out the vegetal flavor.

Serves 1

3 medium carrots

2 ribs celery

1 cup dandelion greens

1 medium Granny Smith apple

Cut all of the ingredients into pieces manageable for your juicer. Juice all the ingredients in the order listed. Stir and enjoy immediately!

Kale, Carrot, Apple, and Ginger Juice

This is a classic juice combination full of vitamins, minerals, and phytochemicals. You can substitute spinach, chard, romaine, or parsley in place of the kale.

Serves 1

4 cups chopped, packed kale, including stems

4 medium carrots

1 medium apple, any variety

1 inch fresh ginger

Cut the ingredients into pieces manageable for your juicer. Juice all the ingredients in the order listed.

Green Pumpkin Spice Smoothie

This smoothie tastes like fall. For added decadence, top it with whipped cream and a sprinkle of cinnamon.

Serves 1

½ cup pumpkin puree

1 (6-ounce) container plain or vanilla yogurt

1 cup packed de-stemmed, chopped kale leaves

½ cup apple juice or cider

½ teaspoon pumpkin pie spice

1 teaspoon honey

Place all the ingredients in a blender, and blend until smooth.

Peaches and Greens

A play on peaches and cream, this smoothie is sweet and refreshing. For extra creaminess, add the heavy cream.

Serves 1

1 cup frozen peaches

1 (6-ounce) container plain yogurt

1 cup packed de-stemmed, chopped kale leaves

1 tablespoon honey

½ cup orange juice

1 tablespoon heavy cream (optional)

Place all the ingredients in a blender, and blend until smooth.

Super Greens Juice

This mild vegetable juice is a lovely maroon color, thanks to the beet and tomato. This is a salad in a glass, especially if you add the balsamic vinegar.

Serves 2

1 small carrot

1 large rib celery

1 cup packed parsley (about 1 bunch)

1 cup packed fresh spinach

2 large kale leaves and stems

½ red beet

2 ripe Roma tomatoes

½ large cucumber

1 teaspoon agave nectar (optional)

1 teaspoon balsamic vinegar (optional)

Cut the ingredients into pieces manageable for your juicer. Juice all the ingredients. For a sweeter flavor, stir in the agave, or for a more savory flavor, stir in the balsamic vinegar. Enjoy immediately!

Greens and Pineapple Juice

This bright green juice is made slightly sweet with the addition of pineapple.

Serves 1

½ medium fresh pineapple,
   peeled
3 cups romaine (about 6
   large leaves)
2 cups packed parsley (about
   2 bunches)
4 cups kale (about 4 large
   leaves)

Cut into pieces manageable for your juicer. Juice each ingredient in the order listed, stir, and enjoy immediately.

Romaine Juice with Carrot, Orange, and Ginger

This juice comes out a bright orange color and tastes just as vibrant, thanks to the ginger. Romaine lettuce has a lot of water in it, so it is great for adding volume.

Serves 1

½ large head romaine
1 large carrot
1 inch fresh ginger
3 medium oranges, peeled

Cut the ingredients into pieces manageable for your juicer. Juice all the ingredients in the order listed. Finishing with the oranges allows all the ginger juice to be extracted. Stir and drink immediately.

Watermelon, Mint, and Spinach Refresher

Imagine drinking this cooling and hydrating juice on a hot summer day or after doing yard work. The spinach turns it a vibrant green. You can use kale, parsley, or chard in place of spinach.

Serves 2

3 cups diced watermelon
3 cups packed fresh spinach
15 large mint leaves
½ medium cucumber
1 cup coconut water

Cut the ingredients into pieces manageable for your juicer. Juice the watermelon, spinach, mint, and cucumber. Stir in the coconut water.

Spinach Smoothie

This energy-packed smoothie makes a great breakfast. It has one serving of vegetables, two-and–a-half servings of fruit, and one serving of dairy.

Serves 1

1 small banana
½ cup plain yogurt
1 cup packed fresh baby spinach
½ cup orange juice
½ cup frozen fruit, such as strawberries, pineapple, or mango

Place the banana, yogurt, spinach, and orange juice in a blender, and pulse until the spinach is well blended. Add the frozen fruit and blend until smooth.

Spinach, Peanut Butter, and Banana Smoothie

This is a classic protein smoothie with added vitamins and fiber from spinach. If you want to cut out some of the fat, use reduced-fat or nonfat yogurt and milk.

Serves 1

1 (6-ounce) container plain yogurt
1 small banana
2 cups packed fresh spinach
3 tablespoons creamy peanut butter
1 tablespoon honey
½ cup 2% or whole milk

Place all the ingredients in a blender, and blend until smooth.

Green Piña Colada Smoothie

The flavors of pineapple and coconut stir up images of sun, sand, and waves. The spinach amps up this smoothie's nutrient value without changing the flavor. If you are in the mood for something a little more adult, add a splash of rum. Orange juice may be substituted for the pineapple juice. If you prefer a sweeter smoothie, add a little honey or agave nectar.

Serves 1

1 cup frozen pineapple chunks
½ cup coconut milk
½ cup pineapple juice
1½ cups packed fresh spinach

Place all the ingredients in a blender, and blend until smooth.

Conversions

Useful Conversions

U.S. MEASURE	EQUIVALENT	METRIC
1 teaspoon	—	5 milliliters
1 tablespoon	3 teaspoons	15 milliliters
1 cup	16 tablespoons	240 milliliters
1 pint	2 cups	470 milliliters
1 quart	4 cups	950 milliliters
1 liter	4 cups + 3½ tablespoons	1000 milliliters
1 ounce (dry)	2 tablespoons	28 grams
1 pound	16 ounces	450 grams
2.21 pounds	35.3 ounces	1 kilogram
270°F / 350°F	—	132°C / 177°C

Volume Conversions

U.S. MEASURE	EQUIVALENT	METRIC
1 tablespoon	½ fluid ounce	15 milliliters
¼ cup	2 fluid ounces	60 milliliters
⅓ cup	3 fluid ounces	90 milliliters
½ cup	4 fluid ounces	120 milliliters
⅔ cup	5 fluid ounces	150 milliliters
¾ cup	6 fluid ounces	180 milliliters
1 cup	8 fluid ounces	240 milliliters
2 cups	16 fluid ounces	480 milliliters

Weight Conversions

U.S. MEASURE	METRIC
1 ounce	30 grams
⅓ pound	150 grams
½ pound	225 grams
1 pound	450 grams

Index